THE

DYNAMIC

PATH

THE
DYNAMIC
PATH

ACCESS THE SECRETS OF CHAMPIONS TO
ACHIEVE GREATNESS THROUGH MENTAL
TOUGHNESS, INSPIRED LEADERSHIP,
AND PERSONAL TRANSFORMATION

JAMES M. CITRIN

RODALE

NOTICE

Mention of specific companies, organizations, or authorities in this book does not imply endorsement by the publisher, nor does mention of specific companies, organizations, or authorities imply that they endorse this book.

Internet addresses and telephone numbers given in this book were accurate at the time it went to press.

© 2007 by James M. Citrin

All rights reserved. No part of this publication may be reproduced or transmitted in any form or by any means, electronic or mechanical, including photocopying, recording, or any other information storage and retrieval system, without the written permission of the publisher.

Rodale books may be purchased for business or promotional use or for special sales. For information, please write to: Special Markets Department, Rodale Inc., 733 Third Avenue, New York, NY 10017.

Printed in the United States of America

Rodale Inc. makes every effort to use acid-free ∞, recycled paper ♻

Book design by Susan Eugster

Illustrations by Ann Williamson and Katie Staun

Library of Congress Cataloging-in-Publication Data

Citrin, James M.

The dynamic path : access the secrets of champions to achieve greatness through mental toughness, inspired leadership, and personal transformation / James M. Citrin.

p.   cm.

Includes bibliographical references and index.

ISBN-13 978–1–59486–358–5 hardcover

ISBN-10 1–59486–358–X hardcover

1. Success in business.   2. Sports.   3. Self-realization.   I. Title.

HF5386.C5757   2007

650.1—dc22   2007024404

Distributed to the trade by Holtzbrinck Publishers

2 4 6 8 10 9 7 5 3 1   hardcover

LIVE YOUR WHOLE LIFE™

We inspire and enable people to improve their lives and the world around them

For more of our products visit rodalestore.com or call 800-848-4735

TO THE BEST FRIENDS

A GUY COULD EVER HAVE:

CLIFF, BARRY, DOUG, ETIENNE,

AND, OF COURSE,

GAIL

Contents

Prologue

Dad, you have to be the most *incompatible* player in the world."

I was playing tennis with my eldest son, Teddy, 15 years old at the time, on some of the best red clay tennis courts in Argentina. I had been a middling Division III college tennis player from 1977 to 1981, but you never would have known it on that Christmas Day in 2005. My forehands were sailing long and my backhands were either sitting up like marshmallows or disappearing meekly into the net. Teddy, who had been ranked as high as number 11 in the New England region of the United States Tennis Association, walked off the court in frustration to join his brother Oliver and their friends for some *good* tennis.

That was a rather humbling moment for me. There I was, in the midst of interviewing, researching, and writing about the greatest champions, coaches, and experts in the wide world of sports with an eye toward gaining breakthrough knowledge about competitive performance in sports and in the workplace. Yet, despite all of the insights that I was picking up, I was not applying *any* of it on the tennis court that day.

That evening, I happened to be editing the transcript from the interview with my childhood hero, Australian tennis legend John Newcombe. I was also reading *The Agassi Story,* the compelling account of how Andre's father, Mike Agassi, channeled his own extraordinary motivation into making his son a tennis champion.

Then it dawned on me. What if I used tennis as my personal laboratory for experimenting with the lessons that I was learning from researching and writing this book? How good a player could I become by the time the book was completed? What changes to my exercise regimen and mental machinations would I have to make? How much of my *40 years* of tennis experience would have to be *undone* in order to improve? And what would this experience imply about the applicability of these lessons to other people and to other parts of my life?

These were intriguing questions that stayed with me over the rest of that family vacation. As I reflected on them, I realized that I could attempt to apply the knowledge while also pursuing my traditional conditioning as well. After all, Agassi, Roger Federer, Rafael Nadal, and all the other great players of today follow rigorous strength, flexibility, and cardio training regimens that keep them strong, flexible, and at the peak of endurance for their tennis (and they don't look too bad either). And now that I was finally unlocking the secrets of mental toughness—that elusive capability to maintain the focus, discipline, and coolness under pressure to win when it counts—I could hopefully make the most out of my own natural talents. To do all of this, I would have to make only two minor adjustments to my life: (1) throw out 25 years of exercise routine[1] to focus on tennis instead, and (2) overcome 40 years of mental and emotional baggage that I had built up about tennis. (For example, the closer I got to winning a match, the more anxious I became. The worse I played, the lower my self-esteem; and the harder I tried to keep the ball in play, the more tentative my shots.) Minor adjustments, indeed.

Where did all that tennis angst come from? When I was growing up in Great Neck, Long Island, in the 1970s, our area was a hotbed of tennis talent and it was intertwined in our social culture. It gave rise to such champions as John McEnroe, who lived in the next town over,

---

[1] From 1981, the year I graduated from college, to that moment at the end of 2005, I had run, biked, and/or swum almost every day, and I faithfully tracked the mileage on a daily, weekly, and annual basis. Over that period, I had traveled a cumulative distance of more than 25,000 miles, long enough to circumnavigate the world.

Douglaston, New York, and Vitas Gerulaitis, from Great Neck. In the 1970s and 1980s, our high school tennis team, Great Neck North, went undefeated year after year and produced two National Collegiate Athletic Association champions and number-one players at Stanford University, several team captains of leading Big Ten and Atlantic Coast Conference universities, and three top-100 ranked players in the world.

I wasn't even close to those demigods. I had the occasional ecstasy of being in "the zone" where the ball obeyed my silent commands. But more often than not, I was afraid to lose. As you surely know, there is no more difficult way to win than to be afraid to lose. That's why I have always been in awe of champions who find a way to pull out an ace, stroke a long putt into the hole, make the three-pointer, or hit the home run at the most crucial moments. They display no fear of losing or fear of winning; they hold nothing back. Not so for me. I had been my own worst enemy.

But that was soon to change. Ever since that memorable day on the red Buenos Aires clay courts, I have conscientiously sought to apply the lessons from this book in my tennis game. More importantly, I have also been incorporating the insights from my research into my day-to-day life at work and at home. It turns out that the findings from conversations with scores of the world's greatest athletic champions, coaches, experts on performance, and other inspiring leaders could readily be applied to my nonsporting life. I strongly believe that the experience of creating this book has enabled me to become a more effective professional and a more fulfilled person. By unearthing and experimenting with the secret to mental toughness in sports, for example, I have found ways to apply that insight in my work at Spencer Stuart and in my role as a father. And by studying how some of the world's most successful performers and greatest leaders continually improve and grow over many years, I've been inspired to set more ambitious short-term and long-range goals. I'm also holding myself to a higher standard, pushing the envelope of my comfort zone, and pursuing important priorities with more discipline and focus.

Today, I have a much deeper understanding of what we can and cannot learn from sports champions and what lessons from athletics are applicable to life outside sports. There is also no doubt in my mind that I have discovered some deeply buried insights into how to become a champion in sports and business and how to live a dynamic and satisfying life as opposed to stagnating and fading into professional and personal oblivion.

Perhaps the most important lesson from this book has been to learn how many different ways there are to make a positive impact on our organizations, our communities, and the world at large. While many of us would love to solve the world's greatest problems, it has become crystal clear to me that you don't have to cure cancer to build a legacy. Nor do you have to be the leader to achieve equal rights for women or minorities or coalesce the world's largest corporations and consumers to eliminate extreme poverty and AIDS in Africa. Happily, others whom I've met over the past 3 years are working specifically toward these noble goals. All that we have to do is follow our own individual calling, pursue it with incredibly hard work, dedication, and excellence, and ensure that it helps other people. That is no more and no less than what is required for each of us to achieve our greatest potential and build a meaningful legacy.

CHAPTER 1

Introduction
The Cloak Room

By 11 o'clock one night, only a few senators remained in the Democratic cloak room. One was writing notes in his folio. Another was pacing back and forth in contemplation. A couple of others were listening attentively to a senior senator pull from his seemingly endless stable of jokes. Another senator—all 6 feet 5 inches of him—stood by the window taking in the whole scene. The anxiousness that he had felt for the previous 4 months as a freshman senator left him at that moment, replaced by a growing sensation of calm. "You know," he thought to himself, "this really isn't a whole lot different from the Knicks' locker room."

His former career as a professional basketball player had given him a wealth of experience from which to draw upon in the US Senate. "It turned out that how I conducted myself in the interpersonal dynamics of the Senate was the same as when I was on the Knicks," Bill Bradley told me some 27 years after that night in the cloak room.

When Bill Bradley began playing basketball in fourth grade in his hometown of Crystal City, Missouri, he did it alone. Bradley's father, a devoted bank manager whose greatest thrill in life was never foreclosing on a customer's home throughout the Great Depression, "didn't even know what basketball was," Bradley says. "He didn't see a basketball game until I was in the seventh grade."

As a teenager, Bradley spent hours upon hours alone in the gym shooting. And shooting. And shooting. He loved the sound of the basketball

1

hitting the polished wooden floor and echoing off of the empty stands. He became addicted to the swish of the ball sailing through the net and the feel of his fingertips in just the right places on the seam of the leather ball. The repetition of dribbling and shooting became a kind of ritual for Bradley. He stayed out on that floor day after day, week after week, year after year. Before he allowed himself to leave the gym each day, he had to make 25 consecutive shots from five different spots around the floor. "Sometimes I would get to 23 and miss the 24th and have to start all over," he said.

Bradley's work ethic was stoked by a comment that he remembers to this day. After his first year in high school, "Easy" Ed McCauley, a former pro basketball player for the Boston Celtics and a local basketball icon in Crystal City, shared words that made a deep impression on the young Bill: "If you're not practicing, just remember—someone somewhere is practicing, and when you two meet, given roughly equal ability, *he* will win."

While Bradley insists that practice makes perfect, he acknowledges that there are some natural gifts that helped make him a basketball star; his height and extraordinary peripheral vision are two. But as Bradley says it, "there is no greater myth in basketball than the 'natural athlete.'" Natural ability, as we will see over and over in this book, can take you only so far.

Not only did he dedicate himself to maximizing his abilities by practicing harder than anyone else, Bradley also loved the team aspect of the game. By the time he made it to Princeton, Bradley felt an overwhelming emotion about his team and a devotion to his teammates: "Something like blood kinship, but without its complications." Bradley took almost perverse joy in "the improbable pass" that made his teammate the star. "It's seeing the pass that leads to the pass that leads to the basket," Bradley says. "When your teammate goes back door because the other guy is overplaying him and you drop a bounce pass perfectly in his hands, arriving at the exact place he needs to get the ball in order to finish the shot and he makes it, it's a transcendent moment. You're then taken someplace out of this world—at least for 5 seconds."

Bradley has always been ambitious both for himself and for the teams and organizations of which he was a member. He was a master at setting concrete goals and pursuing them with focus, action plans, hard work, and dedication. One of the characteristics of Bradley's goals and achievements, similar to most champions, is that they are like building blocks, one resting on top of the other. For example, he wanted his Crystal City High School team to win the Missouri state basketball championship (they did, helping him become a three-time all-American in the process). He wanted his beloved Princeton team to win the (National Collegiate Athletic Association) crown (mission *almost* accomplished; his senior year the team finished number 3 in the NCAA tournament, the best finish in the university's history). Bradley set individual goals as well. He wanted to earn academic honors and become a Rhodes Scholar (he did, and went on to Oxford University's Worcester College for his master's degree). He wanted to earn a spot on the US Olympic team and help the team win a gold medal (not only did he make it, he was elected captain of the 1964 team that indeed won the gold). He wanted to make it into the NBA and be a part of a championship team (his career with the New York Knicks included two NBA championships and election into the Basketball Hall of Fame). He wanted to be elected to the US Senate (his three terms allowed him to serve for 18 years). Finally, he wanted to be elected president of the United States (well, even Bradley couldn't accomplish that one). "The fact that I lost the nomination [in 2000] and therefore lost the chance to be president was a real blow for me," Bradley confided. "But then I realized that it would be foolish to define myself only in terms of being president of the United States. That would be the ultimate form of letting your identity and success be defined from the outside."

3

LAYING THE GROUNDWORK

Not every talented athlete can make it to and succeed in the pros. And not every professional athlete, even the most ambitious, most popular, brightest, and hardest working one, can succeed to the degree of being elected to the US Senate. What made the difference for Bradley? For starters, early in his career he laid the groundwork for his long-term goal of a career in politics and public service. During the off-season, he traveled extensively in the United States and internationally, meeting with social activists, journalists, government officials, academics, and business professionals to expand his knowledge and develop important relationships. He also participated in basketball camps serving disadvantaged youths and taught at the Urban League in Harlem. Beyond New York, Bradley also worked as an assistant to the director of the Office of Economic Opportunity in Washington, D.C., developing a reputation for intelligence and teamwork in influential Democratic circles. In 1978, coupling his reputation as a "thinker" and team player with his popularity from the Knicks, Bradley was able to garner the votes needed to be elected to the US Senate.

With this goal achieved, he set a new one: becoming a highly respected senator known for wise international policies and getting legislation implemented. His attitude and approach were a direct carryover from basketball. Bradley recognized that the objectives were similar: to get people from disparate backgrounds to come together and to cooperate in achieving a common end. He conducted himself in the Senate as he had when he played on the Knicks. "We used to have a joke," he said, "that how a Democrat succeeded in a Republican Senate was to have a good idea and let them steal it." Bradley believes that the improbable pass and its equivalent in a workplace setting is just as rewarding off the court as it was on the court. "If you are truly interested in the success of your endeavor," Bradley says, "then credit is something that you can easily trade away in order to achieve it."

Success rarely falls from the sky and drops in your lap; you generally achieve it in each place you visit, and it grows in your travels along the way. More than 4 decades later, Bradley's Princeton classmates look prescient in retrospect. In their "1965 Senior Class Poll," a half-serious, half-kidding list of 81 different awards, ranging from "Biggest Socialite" and "Most Impeccably Dressed" to "Most Ambitious" and "Most Brilliant," Bradley racked up a few honors that were to foretell his future. He was named "Most Popular," "Best Athlete," "Most Likely to Succeed," and, best of all, "Princeton's Greatest Asset."

An all-American basketball player at Princeton University, Rhodes Scholar, member of the NBA champion team the New York Knicks, long-serving United States senator, and US presidential candidate in the 2000 Democratic primaries. What conceivable relevance could Bill Bradley's career path possibly hold for you or me? Actually, much more than meets the eye.

THE BUILDING BLOCKS OF GREATNESS

Let's start with what it is about Bradley that helped him achieve the goals he set for himself. For starters, credit his natural attributes—Bradley's height, his gifted intellect, and a visual capability that allowed him to "see" the entire court (his peripheral vision allows him to see almost 180 degrees). But how many people with all the brains or physical gifts in the world sputter, only to leave their potential unfulfilled? It was obviously much more than that. Add to his naturally endowed capacities Bradley's prodigious work ethic, which he channeled into highly directed practice. Beyond practicing with his team, he pushed himself in daily personal training sessions, which emphasized repeating *and measuring* important specialized actions that when mastered—the foul shot, the fadeaway jumper, the hook—enabled him to deliver when it counted most in competition.

5

Talent and hard work are a good start. These two attributes are enough to make almost anyone a strong performer in sports, business, law, medicine, or any other field. But what separates the high school star from the professional athlete, and the everyday pro from the Hall of Famer? What is it about the corporate executive that sets him apart from the middle manager, and what prevents that same executive from reaching the rank of top-performing chief executive officer?

To achieve greatness requires something more, something subtle. It demands the acquisition and application of traits common to the most superior performers in sports, business, or any other endeavor: mental toughness and the ability to stay calm and collected at the big moments. In sports, it's called being in the zone. In business, it's having the know-how to get the most important things done when it counts most, thereby delivering the best results. Whether it was on the court for the final shot, in the Senate negotiating rooms during the late-hour brokering sessions to get legislation passed, or in boardrooms coming to terms in final deal points, Bradley has been able to move into the zone, get things done, solve the most difficult problems, and deliver results time and time again at critical moments.

So, are these ingredients—natural ability, hard work, and mental toughness—the secrets to a special formula for greatness? While living by these attributes day in and day out is a proven success formula, it isn't really much of a secret. As I pursued the research for this book, I believed there had to be something else; some undefined qualities that separate the star performers from the rest. I set about searching for those characteristics in order to expand on a set of questions I've been studying for more than a decade. Namely, what does it take to achieve greatness? What are the building block components? Can they be learned, and if so, how?

Over the years, I have addressed these questions first and foremost by interviewing and evaluating many of the world's best business leaders.

Along with a colleague, I also analyzed the work experiences of more than one *million* professionals to distill the patterns of extraordinary careers. But now I wanted a different perspective, and ultimately I decided to study an alternate area of success. Namely, sports. What could I learn from the world's most inspiring athletes? What could be applied from their backgrounds, training regimens, mental disciplines, and competition experiences to help unleash all of the performance potential that resides in each of us? As a lifelong athlete and student of leadership, I was certain that there were hidden linkages between the world's top athletes and the greatest leaders in business. As a corollary, what could I learn from the process of speaking with the world's top athletes to maximize my individual potential and discover my inner— and deeply buried—Olympian?

MASTER CLASS

As a senior partner at Spencer Stuart, my professional life is dedicated to helping leading organizations around the world build their senior leadership teams. A core component of our work involves identifying the most talented leaders in business and developing trust-based relationships based on providing high-value advice on a confidential basis. In our executive search engagements, we work to align our clients' leadership requirements with the skills and aspirations of the most talented and highest-performing leaders. I have always believed that in every significant recruitment, whether recruiting Terry Semel to become chairman and CEO of Yahoo! in 2001, Jon Miller to become chairman and CEO of AOL in 2002, Antonio Perez to become COO (later CEO) of Eastman Kodak in 2003, Dan Glickman to succeed the legendary Jack Valenti as CEO of the Motion Picture Association of America in 2004, Bill Nuti to become CEO of NCR in 2005, Paula Kerger to become CEO of the Public Broadcasting Service in 2006, Joe Uva to become CEO of Univision

Communications in 2007, or any one of the more than 350 other top executives I've recruited, there is a little part of myself left behind as a legacy.

As a complement to my work recruiting top executives, I have long been a dedicated student of leadership and success. I have contributed five books to the canon of the tens of thousands of published works on this subject. Outside of work and intellectual pursuits, I am an athlete and have been my entire life. Starting as an age-group swimmer at 8 years old, performing as a three-sport varsity athlete in both high school and college, and competing as a triathlete, marathoner, golfer, and tennis player as an adult, I have always been passionate about sports and fitness. I have experienced and observed powerful lessons from sports, and now I've studied its relation to performance, both mental and physical, and success in the professional workplace.

We live in a sports-crazed, youth-obsessed, and celebrity-oriented world. With 24/7 exposure magnified by sophisticated marketing, it is no surprise that some of today's heroes are the sports champions whose physical splendor, profound dedication, and icy mental toughness are held up to inspire. And in many cases, inspire they do. Go on, "Be a Tiger." "Put your Lance face on."

There is a lot to learn from great sports leaders, and I've spent hundreds of hours meeting with, speaking to, and watching many of the world's best. I've read thousands of pages of books and articles on their lives, and I've studied some of the most important academic research on peak performance, sports training, the mind-body connection, and the attainment of excellence. I've also analyzed the lives and careers of many of the greatest champions from the past 50 years.

With all of this input poured into a metaphorical centrifuge, I was able to separate out the most powerful insights and isolate those hidden linkages between athletic excellence and professional success. I have to admit that there was a point in my work that was truly disheartening.

For one thing, it turns out that there are precious few surprises about what makes a great athlete. It's all about talent, focus, hard work, dedication, good coaching, and demanding competition. That's about it. Unfortunately, their athletic prowess did not rub off on my always good—but never great—talents. Speaking with Mia Hamm and Joan Benoit-Samuelson did not turn me into a World Cup soccer player or sub-2:30 marathoner. Conversing with Lance Armstrong or Terry Bradshaw didn't bring me closer to riding in the Tour de France or being selected in the NFL draft. Although I did have the privilege of sitting next to Chris Evert at the 2006 US Open and interviewing my boyhood idol, tennis legend John Newcombe, it did not earn me a wild-card entry into Wimbledon. Perhaps most disappointingly, walking along with Tiger Woods at the Masters in April 2006 did not magically help me get up and down from the sand to save par or help me nail that knee-knocking 3-foot birdie putt.

For another thing, try as I might, I could not seem to unearth surprising new breakthroughs about the benefits of sports in life and business. There are many and they are powerful. But they seem to be widely known: learning how to collaborate with others through teamwork, the importance of hard work and discipline, the health benefits of physical exercise and exertion, and the knowledge that young boys and girls who play sports perform better in school, develop greater self-esteem, and have a dramatically lower risk of succumbing to obesity, an issue of crisis proportions in the United States and increasingly in other developed countries as well.

The elusive linkage between great athletic champion and great business leader remained hidden beneath the platitudes. And then it dawned on me . . .

If a genie granted your wish to become the world's best athlete in your favorite sport, what would your *next* wish be? Now, here's where it gets interesting. What would you do with your life if you were 36 years old and recently retired as the leading rusher in NFL history? How about if at the age of 45 you are known around the world as the best rugby player of all time and blessed with the charismatic leadership gene? What if you were declared the greatest tennis player ever and decided to hang up the racquet at 27? Or in a similar vein, what should come next after earning a well-deserved reputation as one of the most respected global citizens of our modern era, and hanging up the boots after a career in the US Army and having served as the chairman of the Joint Chiefs of Staff and US secretary of state?

I've been about as close to being that genie as it gets. Over the past 3 years, I have discovered that the answers to these "what next" questions are most assuredly not obvious. I learned that the link I sought wasn't to be found in any singular attribute or action. Life isn't quite that straight-forward. Instead, what I discovered was a process, a path. And what became clear is that the path to greatness is not static; it demands change and adaptation, learning and learning some more, letting go of the skills and actions that led to achievement at one level and developing new ones. It requires learning how to lead and inspire others and directing your efforts to a deeply meaningful cause. It is The Dynamic Path.

ON THE STREETS OF NEW YORK

The New York Road Runners (NYRR) is the nation's largest running club, hosting 55 events a year across the city's five boroughs. Its signature event is the ING New York City Marathon, which began humbly in 1970 with a $1,000 budget and just 55 finishers and has become an annual festival that attracts 30,000 runners from around the world and brings out 12,000 volunteers and more than two million cheering spectators to the city streets. Runners cover the gamut—from the sport's best men, who cover the demanding 26.2-mile course in under 2 hours and 10 minutes, and the world's best women, who clock about 2:24, to firefighters, office workers, students, teachers, doctors, nurses, and retirees who have trained for months to achieve their goal of completing this race.

Mary Wittenberg became president and CEO of NYRR and race director of the ING New York City Marathon in April 2005, the first woman ever to oversee a major city marathon. Today, sitting atop the world's largest running club, a not-for-profit organization that boasts 40,000 members and a $30 million operating budget, the intelligent, athletic 45-year-old is coming into her own as a leader. A hard-nosed attorney with a background in corporate law, she also was a world-class distance runner who qualified for the Olympic Trials in the marathon event. With her professional experience as a law firm partner and elite running credentials, Wittenberg was recruited to NYRR in 1998 as executive vice president of administration.

In her office, atop an Upper East Side townhouse, Wittenberg said excitedly, "Big news. Lance Armstrong has decided to run the NYC (2006) Marathon this year. The marathon will be a bigger draw than ever with Lance in our ranks since he epitomizes the spirit of the marathon." Wittenberg is evangelical as she describes the New York City Marathon. "It is a celebration of life at its finest, with tens of thousands of runners striving to overcome hurdles and achieve great personal goals, using the support of millions of spectators. It reinforces our efforts to get people moving toward healthier and fitter lives."

Wittenberg was the first child in a large family in Buffalo, New York. She and her six siblings played baseball, softball, and basketball, both with each other and in local leagues, with their father coaching many of the teams. In her senior year of high school, after 3 years of cheerleading, Wittenberg decided to become a more active athletic participant. She found the perfect opportunity at the West Side Rowing Club on Lake Erie, which happens to be the largest rowing club in the United States. She took to crew instantly, dedicating the next 5 years to the sport. Her lean build, long limbs, and stellar coordination gave her a natural ability on the water.

Wittenberg attended Canisius College in Buffalo and continued rowing with the West Side Rowing Club. She was also selected as a freshman to become coxswain for the men's college crew team. The job of the cox is to be a leader, coach, and motivator for her rowing teammates; it was a breakthrough position for a woman at the time. The team's daily training schedule included demanding runs, and Wittenberg more than held her own with her male teammates. Her ability to keep pace with the boys not only boosted her status on the team, it sparked a lifelong love of running, which ultimately led to a memorable road racing career.

On a night out with friends during her senior year of college, Wittenberg accepted a challenge to run a road race being held the following day. To her own surprise, she went out and won. Her performance caught the eye of Canisius's cross-country coach, who approached her after the race and suggested she give his team a try. She demurred. But he persisted: "Try it for two weeks. If you don't love it, go ahead and quit." Wittenberg accepted his offer and, indeed, fell in love with the sport. She trained with the men's team for the rest of her senior year and culminated her season by winning the Diet Pepsi 10-K Road Race Series in Buffalo, which qualified her to race against the best in the country in New York City.

After graduating in 1984, Wittenberg went to South Bend, Indiana, to begin law school at the University of Notre Dame. Again, she found a way to train with the best, having been invited by Coach Joe Piane to run with the university's men's cross-country team. This experience gave Wittenberg a foundation of friendship, camaraderie, and mutual respect (not universally present in law school) that allowed her to create collegial bonds with men, an ability that she says has served her well throughout her professional career. While training with this group, Wittenberg decided to run the 1985 Chicago Marathon. Mary lined up next to champions Joan Benoit, Ingrid Kristiansen, and Rosa Mota. "It was incredibly exciting," she recalls. With stern instructions from Coach Piane to run conservatively, Wittenberg finished the course in a blistering 2:46, earning her a 16th-place finish with energy to spare.

At the end of law school, Wittenberg decided to work for a large law firm in a smaller city, with the goal of becoming a top partner in a major corporate law practice. She joined the firm Hunton & Williams in its Richmond, Virginia, office. Coincidentally, the head of the corporate group who recruited her also was a runner. He encouraged her to leave work at 3:30 every afternoon to train. Just as she did in South Bend, Wittenberg joined up with the top local runners, this time with the University of Richmond cross-country team. After her workouts, Wittenberg returned to the office and studied for the bar exam or worked until the wee hours of the morning. "I was burning the candle at both ends trying to walk the line between my work and running. I could have easily ended up injuring myself and failing the bar." As it turned out, she passed the bar exam in the first sitting and her running became better than ever. In 1987, she won the Marine Corps Marathon in 2:44, earning her a spot at the 1988 Olympic Trials.

The Marine Corps Marathon, however, proved to be Wittenberg's running peak, as the demanding schedule of legal work and Olympic training took its toll. Just 11 weeks before the Olympic Trials, she injured her knee and had to undergo surgery. Then a week before the race, she was further debilitated with a back injury. Though she started the race, she was forced to drop out after only 2 miles. She shed tears of anguish and disappointment, which were broadcast by news media across the United States.

Over the next several years, with her serious running career behind her, Wittenberg dove into work at her law firm with the same devotion she used in her training. In 1994, she moved to New York City with her firm, a move that pushed running to the back seat in order to maintain the ferocious pace of corporate legal work in the big city. Despite the professional demands, however, she did find a way to hook up with several running teams in the area, and in the process met her future husband, Derek. Her dedication and performance at work were rewarded in 1997 when she became the first woman to make partner at her firm.

Having earned the brass ring, Wittenberg felt a bit hollow, not unlike many others who achieve a long-sought-after goal only to question if the goal was worth the pursuit. "I got to the point where I knew I was not put on this earth to do tax-driven corporate transactions," she says.

In the summer of 1998, Allan Steinfeld, president of the New York Road Runners, was looking for a "number two" for the organization. The club was still recovering and reorganizing after the death of Fred Lebow, the renowned founder of the New York City Marathon and longtime president of the New York Road Runners. "Fred was Mr. Outside," says Wittenberg. "He was the visionary and Allan was the execution guy, the brilliant tactician. When Fred died [of brain cancer], Allan tried to do both jobs during a time when the club was growing at an amazing rate. All of a sudden, it had become a multimillion-dollar operation. There was this tremendous need at the club, which I found extremely attractive."

The club agreed, offering Wittenberg the job of executive vice president of administration, the highest position a woman had held in the club's history. In 2000, she became the organization's first-ever chief operating officer, responsible for overseeing NYRR's business, operations, administration, event production, the NYRR Web site, *New York Runner* magazine, merchandise, membership, and race scoring. She took to the role like a duck to water. "It was a daunting and exhilarating time," Wittenberg says about her first months on the job. "I realized pretty quickly that this was my dream job, working to promote a sport I love. I've never looked back for a second."

Leaders in the running community have lauded Wittenberg's skill and impact. "Mary is simply terrific," says Olympic gold medalist Joan Benoit-Samuelson. "She gets things done, creates exciting goals, works well with others, and has been tremendous for our sport." Part of Wittenberg's effectiveness derives from her authenticity and the alignment of her work with her life goals. "I really appreciate the opportunity to make a difference," Wittenberg says. "Running changes people's lives at all levels."

Mary Wittenberg is a relatively ordinary person who has accomplished extraordinary things. She is having a positive impact on thousands of other people as she helps them live their lives to the fullest. Wittenberg is like thousands of others who have worked incredibly hard, grown, adapted, aligned their roles with their strengths and passions, and found themselves succeeding in leadership roles. While not a household name, Wittenberg is every bit the role model Bill Bradley is. Mary Wittenberg is a prime example of The Dynamic Path in action.

THE DYNAMIC PATH

By understanding and traveling The Dynamic Path, you may well achieve greatness beyond your own expectations or even beyond your dreams. The inherent force throughout the process, not surprisingly, is *dynamism,* an energy that drives change, vigor, and progress. Dynamism is by definition a fluid system, the opposite of static. The Dynamic Path is the course that Bradley, Wittenberg, and many others in this book have followed to progress, transforming themselves as well as the people, organizations, and institutions around them. It is one thing to be a star individual contributor in sport or life. It is quite another to extend beyond oneself, to work with and through others.

Look past the overt declarations of natural ability and unstoppable work ethic. Beyond them, you find the elements of The Dynamic Path—

principles that guide the world's most successful athletes forward. They are the very same principles that lead others to success in business, science, public service, and life in general. These principles are to:

▶ **Grow or perish.** You need to grow continually as a person by learning and developing new skills.

▶ **Build on experiences and accomplishments.** It is imperative to find ways to apply your experiences to new situations in order to create new opportunities for the future.

▶ **Focus on the success of others.** When you are dedicated to making those around you successful, success will accrue as a natural end result.

▶ **Play to your strengths and interests.** It is essential to become ever more aware of what it is that you are really good at and find a way to make that strength the core of your work. Strengths also become magnified when they are applied in a field where you are genuinely interested in the topic at hand.

▶ **Find a worthy and relevant cause.** Whether on a historic scale like battling to cure cancer, a large scale like helping inner-city youth find a way out, or on a smaller scale like becoming a mentor, the more you isolate something genuinely meaningful to you that is worth fighting for, the more your people, moral, and spiritual leadership will hurtle you along the path to success.

These are the principles themselves, the features of the path that the most accomplished leaders follow. But what is the path itself?

The Dynamic Path is a series of three-way points, each culminating at a momentous decision point, the "Dynamic Moment":

▶ Stage I—*The Champion.* This is the stage where individual accomplishment is achieved for individual results; the highest form of ability is to perform as an individual.

▶ Stage II—*The Great Leader.* This is the stage where collective achievement is realized for collective results; the highest form of ability is to perform as a group.

▶ Stage III—*The Legacy.* This is where collective achievement is attained for enduring results; the highest form of ability is to impact future individual and group performance.

In its simplest form, The Dynamic Path looks like this:

The Dynamic Path and Its Core Components

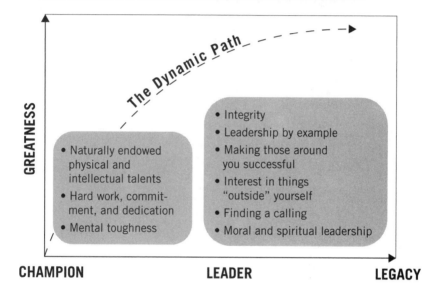

Throughout this book, we will explore the components of The Dynamic Path and you will come to know many individuals, both household names and otherwise, who will bring the path to life. The big payoff will be to help you figure out what this all implies for *you*, how you can achieve your greatest aspirations and attain your ultimate potential.

Two words of caution: First, please, do not get discouraged as you read through the stories in this book. While it might be tempting to feel some degree of diffidence relative to the inspiring achievements of extraordinary individuals, the fact is that exceptional results and meaningful impact are yours for the taking. Second, if you are enamored by underlying frameworks and theory, the next chapter, which takes a deeper dive into the mechanics of The Dynamic Path, is for you. If you are inclined to just get on with it, however, please accept my invitation to skim and move swiftly ahead to Chapter 3.

CHAPTER 2

A Touch of Immortality

The Dynamic Path Explained

Many find it surprising that former US secretary of state Madeleine Albright was a member of the Wellesley College swimming and diving team. Or that Vera Wang, CEO of the fashion design company that bears her name, was a world-class figure skater. Jan Leschly was once much better known as the 10th-ranked men's tennis player in the world and for representing his native Denmark in the Davis Cup than he ever was as the CEO of pharmaceutical giant SmithKline Beecham. Those who know her are actually *not* surprised to learn that eBay's CEO, Meg Whitman, played collegiate lacrosse and squash at Princeton University. But when witnessing the United Nations General Assembly at work, some found it hard to picture former secretary general Kofi Annan running track and playing soccer at Macalester College in St. Paul, Minnesota.

Surprising as these examples may be, many of the skills and qualities that led these and other leaders to success in professional life were initially developed in playing sports.

Louise Ritter, US gold medalist in high jump in the 1988 Olympics, once said, "If you are disciplined enough to fight for something in the sports world, then you will be disciplined enough to be successful in the business world. Once you have been a winner [in sports], you [rightfully] believe you can be a winner in everything you do."

There have long been highly successful business professionals and executives whose competitive streak was molded on the athletic pitch.

Today, business success and sports performance at the elite level often go hand in hand. The list of top executives who are single-digit-handicap golfers, Ironman triathletes, champion yachtsmen, ranked tennis and squash players, even chess grandmasters is getting longer. There are even televised CEO fishing tournaments and CEO golf challenges to go along with the regularly published rankings of business leaders and their respective performance across different sports.

Many of the same underlying factors that lead to sports success result in similar outcomes in the business arena. Most executives are highly competitive, ambitious, energetic, goal-oriented people who love to put points on the board no matter what the setting. As we'll see, applying these and other qualities contributes to making a champion in sports and in business. Does this mean that abysmal coordination shuts you out of the top ranks of business? Certainly not. However, many of the qualities that top performers in business exhibit are also on clear display on the sporting fields. Learn from them and your professional success will undoubtedly be enhanced.

THE SPECIAL QUALITY OF SPORTS

Participation in sports and fitness has multiple benefits for people of all ages. Young athletes who play organized sports benefit from increased self-esteem and motivation, dedication, resilience, decisiveness, and confidence—essential ingredients in the development of future leaders. Studies show that young student-athletes earn better grades, have fewer problems outside school, have better attendance, and drop out far less frequently than their non-athlete classmates.

Not that sports are unique in their ability to develop leadership attributes. Other competitive collaborative activities, such as theater, dance troupes, science fairs, debate teams, and the military build them up as well. But there's something special about the physicality of sports and fitness. Those who exercise regularly know the manifold benefits of remaining active and keeping in shape. Scientific evidence shows that exercise provides a short-term increase in people's ability to process data. Exercise has also been shown to reduce depression and anxiety, illnesses that can hamper the functioning of the brain. Over the long term, exercise has also been shown to help prevent the mental and physical effects of aging. For these reasons, sports are a good place to start along The Dynamic Path. However, make no mistake: There are also many examples of individuals outside of sports who exhibit the champion, leader, and legacy qualities that we will be reviewing.

FROM INDIVIDUAL TO CHAMPION, FROM LEADER TO LEGACY

While there are many different routes to success, there are commonalities among those followed, knowingly or unknowingly, by the very best performers. It often starts with a straight shot from natural talent to ambitious goal setting to intense pursuit to superb achievement. However, more often than not, genuine greatness can be attained only when dramatic difficulties must be confronted and overcome. Inevitably, things take a detour just about the moment when it all seems to be figured out.

The first step to greatness begins when one thrives by applying one's naturally endowed talent. Through dedication, hard work, and mental toughness the individual grows to achieve excellence in his or her field. In the world of sports, the best of the best become champions, bathed in positive attention from friends, teammates, and fans. But no matter how celebrated a person becomes at a moment in time, most champions fade away after their time in the sun. Those few who manage to stay on top do so by continuing to grow and develop as individuals and as leaders.

Like the homecoming kings and queens whose lives peak in high school, there are few things more depressing than the washed-up athlete who lives in the glory days of the past. By contrast, witnessing vibrant, motivated, and principled sports champions who learn from their achievements and apply those lessons to create new opportunities for themselves and for others is inspiring. Those are the individuals who go on to have the most significant impact on others and the world around them.

Arthur Ashe, for example, the first African American man to win a Grand Slam men's singles title in tennis, was one such individual. Nearly 15 years after his untimely 1993 death from a blood transfusion infected with HIV, the very mention of Ashe still elicits feelings of reverence. James Blake, one of the world's best tennis players, has called Arthur Ashe a role model not just to tennis players but to all people in every sense of the word. Blake, who at the time of this writing is not only the highest-ranked African American but the number 9 ranked player in the world, was quoted in the *New York Times* saying, "Ashe overshadowed his amazing tennis career with being a much more admirable person. That is a goal I believe that any person can look up to and aim for."

Ashe was one of tennis's greatest ambassadors, both on and off the court. After his historic victory as the first African American to win the US Open in 1968, he went on to win 33 titles in his career, including the Australian Open in 1970 and Wimbledon in 1975. He also devoted countless hours to creating tennis opportunities for youth of all backgrounds. In 1969, for example, Ashe cofounded the USA National Junior Tennis League (NJTL), a program to provide youth from low-income neighborhoods the opportunity to learn tennis. Ever since, he has served as a beacon for African American tennis players, including Venus and Serena Williams, who both took part in the NJTL when they were learning the game. Off the court, Ashe worked tirelessly to eliminate racism and poverty around the world, particularly during the apartheid era in South Africa. Through his work and example, Arthur Ashe made the world a much better place.

THE ULTIMATE DESTINATION

Lance Armstrong, arguably the most recognized athlete on the planet, thanks to his inspirational recovery from cancer and the inconceivable feat of winning the Tour de France a record seven consecutive times, said that his life goal is to be remembered less for his cycling exploits and more for his work helping to cure cancer. As the May 8, 2006, cover of *Sports Illustrated* trumpeted, "Attacking his new career like he did the Tour de France and closing ground on cancer, Lance is becoming a political force unlike any other athlete in history."

And so it goes, from Arthur Ashe and Lance Armstrong to Billie Jean King and Mia Hamm to Tiger Woods and Tony Hawk to Magic Johnson. Those who have established legacies, the ultimate destination on The Dynamic Path, have contributed far beyond themselves and even beyond their sport to the world around them.

The chart below shows how The Dynamic Path works, depicting how you progress from individual to champion, and evolve from leader to legacy.

The Dynamic Path

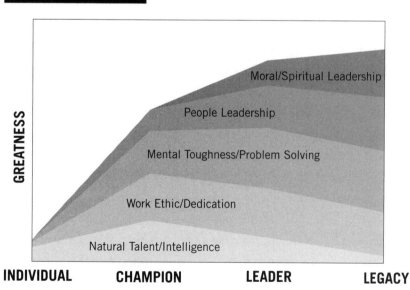

Time and the principal stages through which one travels along The Dynamic Path grace the horizontal axis. The vertical axis is a relative scale of greatness. Let's take a look into each of the stages.

THE MAKING OF A CHAMPION

Just as a great CEO starts as a superb individual contributor in business, an individual becomes a sports champion first by becoming a great athlete. Three principal factors work together to make a great athlete: natural physical talent, dedication and a potent work ethic, and mental toughness.

Those who become great athletes typically begin with naturally endowed athletic talent. This takes the form of speed, agility, hand-eye coordination, endurance, strength, flexibility, quickness, jump reach, balance, and any of another myriad attributes. Tens of thousands if not millions of youngsters have such talents. The second factor, consisting of dedication and consistent hard work, quickly separates fun-loving kids playing sports around the house and in town leagues from committed athletes. Their work ethic expands to a point nearing obsession.

Committed athletes sharpen their skills through highly directed practice. Like Andre Agassi, they hit hundreds of returns of serve and backhand approach shots a day; like Bill Bradley, they shoot dozens of shots from each point around the key; or like Grant Hackett, a world-record holder and captain of the Australian national swim team, they swim 10,000 or more yards of interval training on a daily basis. They stretch every day, strengthen every other day, and envision competitive situations constantly. Together with the discipline required to keep up this regimen, the support of high-quality coaching, and an encouraging home, team, or community environment, top performers become great athletes by also developing a third attribute: mental toughness.

Mental toughness allows an individual to thrive when it counts most, remaining cool, calm, and collected during the ups and downs of a game, race, match, or tournament. It is that skill that allows an athlete to play in an instinctive and automatic way at the turning points of a competition. How do they do it? Mentally tough athletes create an environment in which their opponents—and not themselves—crack under pressure. How can *you* do it? Chapter 3 will unlock the secrets.

There is a fine line between a great athlete and a champion. At its most basic level, a champion is a person who competes in and wins a competition. But a true champion goes beyond winning. For me, at least, a champion embodies excellence and achievement over a sustained period of time. The champion may not win every time, but losing is the rarer of the two, and peak performance and all-out effort are the constants.

We all watched in awe when Michael Jordan hit nothing but the net for another game-winning three-pointer, when Roger Federer gracefully outdueled another opponent on his way to a major title, when Tiger Woods made the crucial shot on Sunday afternoon for another tournament victory, or when Lance Armstrong powered to another seminal Tour de France win. These are champions.

Becoming a champion requires that a great athlete continue developing his or her physical capabilities and technical talent in his or her sport. This typically takes the form of at least a decade of highly focused, or "directed," practice. On the chart on page 23, notice that the work ethic, mental toughness, and natural talent layers thicken until they reach their deepest point at the moment when one becomes a champion. The thicker the layer, the greater the capability. In other words, in order for individuals to continue to improve, they must increase their skills, working harder and exercising greater dedication than ever before. Dedication and hard work are consistent ingredients all along The Dynamic Path, from champion to leader to legacy. Similarly, mental toughness never loses its importance. As we'll see through the stories in this book, champions also have the resilience to face whatever life—never mind a competition—throws at them.

While natural talent peaks at the same time as mental toughness and work ethic, its influence on the developing leader wanes. Just as athletic gifts fade over time, so too do the benefits and importance of individual achievement. Individual champions move into the background. Champions are those who come through for their teams and themselves when the stakes are highest. The greatest champions, however, go beyond merely delivering at the moment of truth. Based on their leadership by example, their commitment, work ethic, values, and integrity, they become an inspiration for others on and off the court or field.

THE MAKING OF A GREAT LEADER

Whether in sports, business, government, or any other field, the core elements of leadership are consistent and timeless. Hundreds of thousands of pages have been written on the topic, but at its core, leadership is simply the ability to inspire others to achieve great things. In my earlier research on leadership, fully 90 percent of the most extraordinary business leaders (the top 10 percent of the most senior 1 percent of American executives) are described as "caring as much about the success of those who work with and for them as their own success," while only 4 percent of this extraordinary group are described as putting themselves first. By contrast, among the broad population of senior managers, 40 percent of those considered average performers are described as putting themselves first.[1]

---

[1] Based on research performed in 2002 for *The Five Patterns of Extraordinary Careers*; survey of 2,000 senior-level executives in the United States that extrapolate to the most senior one million executives +/–3 percent.

The most successful individuals populating the top levels of organizations are those who attract the top talent and inspire them to exceptional levels of performance. They create an environment where the very best performers want to work, will perform at peak levels, and will remain loyal to the organization. When we examined the experiences of hundreds of the highest-performing business leaders, it was apparent that they were the beneficiaries of the talents and performance of their peers, subordinates, and superiors.

In the case of sports leaders, this may take the form of the quarterback or coach calling the final play in the time-out with seconds to play and inspiring the team to make the touchdown for the win. Or it may be the soccer midfielder who sets up the winning goal by outhustling her opponent and breaking free for the perfect cross. Bill Bradley describes it in the following way: "It's easy to spot the team leader," he says. "He's the one whom the team looks to get the ball to in the final seconds of the game." This isn't due solely to that individual's ability to shoot. It's much more profound than that. It has to do with trust that is built up over time through leading by example and delivering when it counts.

At some point for people in sports, physical ability will ebb and athletic talents will fade. This is a dynamic moment—a critical life-turning point. Some ignore the telltale signals and seek to hang on and ride out their careers, working hard to maintain the skills that got them to their peak. Others decide to confront the moment and change. Through continued hard work and commitment, the mental discipline to adapt to their changing situation, and a relentless focus on making others around them successful, the champion can continue to grow as a person and as a leader. On the chart on page 23, you can see that the people leadership layer expands more rapidly than the natural talent layer declines. This depicts the dynamic change necessary to continue growing.

If, on the other hand, an accomplished competitor remains focused on him- or herself and tries to rely principally on natural or physical talents, it is inescapable that the champion will become a former champion and will ultimately fade into oblivion. As plotted on the chart, this would be depicted as the people leadership layer not expanding to offset the inevitable decline of natural talent.

Remember Dick Barnett, Bill Bradley's teammate on the NBA-champion New York Knicks? He spent 14 years in the NBA and was a part of the legendary 1970 Knicks team that won the league championship. After his retirement in 1974, he tried his hand at a variety of jobs. One was selling investments, hoping to take advantage of his identity as a Knick to open doors and generate accounts. Despite the best of intentions, this did not work out too well. He relied on the single dimension of his pro-basketball identity, ignoring the new skills that would have been required to succeed in this unrelated field. Happily, later in his post-basketball career, Barnett found a more natural application for his experience, which also benefited others—teaching sports management at St. John's University in New York.

Joe Torre, by contrast, didn't need an interim step to move from champion to leader. He thrived as a player and then applied his experience directly for the benefit of others, including players and fans. A nine-time All-Star playing for the St. Louis Cardinals, Torre was one of the best catchers of all time. He became manager of the New York Yankees in 1995, and his record is astounding. Torre led the Yankees to the playoffs in each of his 11 seasons with the team. He managed the Yankees to four World Series wins, including 1996, the team's first championship since 1978, and three World Series wins in a row from 1998 to 2000. Under his stewardship, the Yankees clinched the American League championships in 2001 and 2003.

Torre cemented his place in the pinstriped pantheon as an inspirational leader, a cool strategist under pressure, and a person of unquestioned integrity. He even found the formula to work successfully with a legendarily difficult boss, George Steinbrenner.

✦

GE's Jeffrey Immelt—
Leadership Through Learning

Speaking of big-time bosses, consider Jeffrey Immelt, the dynamic CEO of General Electric, the most admired company on the planet. At the core of Immelt's leadership philosophy is a simple concept: The basis for success is not how much you know, but how quickly you can learn. This is leadership through learning.

Immelt himself had to learn the CEO ropes quickly. His first day as the ninth chairman and chief executive officer in GE's history was relatively calm. His second day was September 11, 2001. Learn quickly he did. During his 6 years at the helm, Immelt has guided GE in reshaping its business portfolio, making landmark acquisitions in health care and entertainment, reducing the company's dependence on financial services, and ushering in a global focus on being environmentally responsible. He has also made important organizational and management changes and has been a driving force in reforming executive compensation, including his own, to be more closely linked to company and stock performance. As a result, similar to his predecessors in the GE corner office, Immelt proved to be a herald of management ideas and practices for other companies to follow.

Immelt began his GE career in 1982, and, in the 25 years since then, he has held global leadership roles in GE's plastics, appliance, and medical businesses. Learning has been key to his business success from the beginning, thanks to the foundation his parents laid. "They believed that a good education was the great social equalizer, something that stays with you your whole life and that allows anyone to live their dreams. At GE, I have the chance to see real learning and continuous improvement in action around the company and at Crotonville [GE's famed training center]."

He believes there is a direct link between learning and leadership. Immelt and his managers consider the ability to learn and learn quickly to be a key prerequisite to promotion. This attribute is a major reason for the success of the most accomplished business leaders, in Immelt's view. "Almost every great CEO whom I've met," he says, "is focused on continual learning."

Immelt, who played varsity football at Dartmouth College, also appreciates the role sports and other competitive collaborative activities play in the making of a leader. "I think it's huge," he says. "Sports combine a bunch of important things: competitiveness, teamwork, knowing when to lead and when to follow, and dealing with both success and failure. I think competitive, collaborative activities, of which sports is the prime example, help shape the very important skill sets for the business world. We look for people who have had teaming kind of events, such as the military, sports, or theater, activities that have forced people into group situations and made them learn how to collaborate and compete. So I think sports are just great."

THE MAKING OF A LEGACY

Newton's first law of motion states that "an object at rest tends to stay at rest, and an object in motion tends to stay in motion with the same speed and in the same direction unless acted upon by an unbalanced force." The natural tendency of things and objects, therefore, is to resist changes in their state of motion. This is called *inertia*. By analogy, despite all the challenges that are present in our lives today, it is still very difficult to change the status quo, even if you are trying to make change for the better. But the champion who grows into a great leader of people has the skills, visibility, access, and power to do just that. It's largely a matter of focus. The inspiring individuals who dedicate themselves to a particular cause—or calling—that is meaningful to them and valuable to others in their communities and in society at large create the opportunity to leave a legacy and, in the process, achieve their ultimate potential.

Skateboarding king Tony Hawk is a great champion who has set up a meaningful organization to support the greater good. One of the heroes of America's youth, Hawk is reportedly the second-most-recognized athlete in the United States. To give back and build an enduring legacy, he created the Tony Hawk Foundation, which funds skateparks in communities across the country, providing a place for young people to be outdoors skating, getting exercise, and engaging with others. The foundation's board focuses on providing skatepark grants to low-income areas that have a high percentage of at-risk youth and whose communities demonstrate a strong grassroots commitment to the project.

FOR TIGER, "GOLF IS WHAT I DO, NOT WHO I AM"

When *60 Minutes* introduced its segment on Tiger Woods in March 2006, the voice-over intoned, "Tiger is the type of athlete who comes along not once in a generation, but perhaps once in the history of a sport. For the last decade, he has dominated professional golf so completely that he has changed the game."

How can Tiger Woods possibly handle the pressures of competing against the world's best week in and week out and maintain his winning ways? According to renowned golf coach, sports psychologist, and best-selling author Robert "Dr. Bob" Rotella, PhD, the answer lies beyond his magical natural talent, his unsurpassed dedication and hard work, and his ice-in-the-veins mental toughness. It has to do with his raison d'être for winning, which was given to him by his father. "The most important thing that Earl Woods did for Tiger," Dr. Rotella says, "was telling him from a very early age, 'I want you to be the greatest player in history so you can change race relations around the world.'" In other words, he gave Tiger an important calling greater than himself, even greater than the game of golf. "I think that has been huge philosophically," Dr. Rotella says. "It has taken away Tiger's fear of losing, and more importantly, his fear of winning. It has also taken away the pressures of notoriety." It's all about wanting to be well known and well respected so that he can lead by example and influence others to do the right things.

Dr. Rotella continues, "If you think about how well he has handled himself, what he's accomplished at such a young age, it's mind-boggling. Think about how easy it would be to be in love with himself with that much success. I think so many other sports have athletes that have blown the opportunity to be a role model."

Tiger is well on his way not only to building an enduring legacy in golf, where he is on track to win the most majors ever, but in society at large as well. In 1996, he and his father established the Tiger Woods Foundation to inspire and empower young people across America to "strive for excellence and realize their potential." Over the past decade, the foundation has helped many thousands of kids through personal development programs, scholarships, direct grants, junior golf teams, and most importantly, the Tiger Woods Learning Center (TWLC).

Conceived in 2002 and opened in 2006, the TWLC is a state-of-the-art 35,000-square-foot, 14-acre education center in Anaheim, California. Built as a unique after-school curriculum rooted in science, math, and language, the center offers students such courses as computer science, forensic science, creative writing, and rocketry—all subjects that they said they wanted.

"This is so near and dear to my heart," Tiger said, referring to providing education, inspiration, and opportunities for young people to achieve their goals and dreams. "It's more important than any golf shot that I can possibly hit."

"Golf is what I do," Tiger said. "It is definitely not who I *am*."

A TOUCH OF IMMORTALITY

The underlying desire to create a legacy does not spring from magnanimity alone. Like the quest for spiritual understanding, people worldwide have a deep-seated urge to be meaningful contributors to the world. "Given the awareness of our mortality," said Jeffrey Greenberg, PhD, a University of Arizona psychologist, "in order to function securely, we need to feel somehow protected from the existential predicament, to feel like we are more than just material animals fated only to obliteration upon death. We accomplish that by trying to view ourselves as enduringly valuable contributors to a meaningful world. And the more others validate our value, the more special and therefore secure we can feel."

When one decides to focus his or her attention on a particular calling or mission that will make a discernible positive impact on the world, a leader comes to that third dynamic moment—the decision to build a legacy. If the cause is worthy and if there is a credible reason for selecting it as well as a wholesome way of pursuing it that resonates with others, then the opportunity arises for a person to become a moral or even spiritual leader. During one's lifetime, like Lance Armstrong, or sometimes afterward, like Arthur Ashe, a legacy is established by tapping into the emotions and aspirations of a broad population.

✦

Bud Greenspan—
Chronicler of the Olympic Games

How can you build an enduring legacy from a career in sports *without* being an athlete? By following the example of Bud Greenspan. He is the world's foremost writer, producer, and director of sports films and one of the leading sports historians. He has received seven Emmy Awards and the Olympic Order from the International Olympic Committee and is also regarded as the closest thing to the official chronicler of the modern Olympic Games.

In his *100 Years of Olympic Glory*, Greenspan wrote that "it will be to the everlasting glory of our time that there came forth at the end of the 19th century a man with a grand vision: to revive an ideal that had its beginning thousands of years ago, in ancient Greece. When asked why he renewed the Olympic Games, founder Baron de Coubertin replied, 'To ennoble and strengthen sport.'"

Greenspan's films focus less on celebrating champions than on saluting lesser-known athletes who have overcome obstacles to compete with dignity and honor. He has long demonstrated an uncanny knack for capturing the human drama of sports, for showcasing the human spirit. "I don't make films about superheroes and sports stars," Greenspan said. "I make films about people. People who experience hard work, joy and sorrow, success and failure, just like anyone else." How about the lessons from Olympic champions? "We often learn more about human drive, love, and determination from those coming in sixth than from those coming in first."

With his comprehensive perspective on athletic achievement, what is Bud Greenspan's definition of greatness? Bud says that he has personally been most moved by those special athletes who have inspired people both on and off the playing field. There are four specific things that he most admires about athletes he's covered: talent, pride, courage, and most important, the ability to endure. "The biggest thing that I've learned in my life from the greatest athletes is to stay in the arena, to keep from being a spectator."

THE DYNAMIC PATH IS NOT FOR EVERYONE

Some people set precise long-term goals and construct detailed action plans to try to achieve them. Others are fatalistic about how their life unfolds and are resigned to let events take their course. There are others still who decide to live by a set of principles and try not to focus on outcomes. The number of ways to move from point "A" to point "B" in life is unlimited, and there are infinite gradations between striving for control and letting it be. The Dynamic Path—working to become a champion, evolving into a great leader, and ultimately building and leaving behind a legacy—is only one way.

After all, not everyone wants to be or is prepared to make the sacrifices to become a champion in sports or a star performer in business. Not everyone wants to assume the responsibilities of leadership or to focus on the success of others around them. And while many people want something that will outlive them and provide a modicum of evidence of a life meaningfully lived, not everyone has the drive or passion to create a bequest of significance. But for those who aspire to do all of these things, The Dynamic Path is the way. While no one can guarantee you a global legacy like Arthur Ashe, The Dynamic Path is a way of enrichment and continual personal development, and a road to greatness.

Some may choose to aspire to a single stage along The Dynamic Path. Nothing says that a champion has to continue in the same vein and build directly on his or her success to become an inspirational leader. Eric Heiden achieved what Bud Greenspan called the greatest feat in Olympic history. In 1980 at Lake Placid, he won five individual gold medals in speed-skating and set Olympic records in each and every event, from the sprint 500-meter to the marathon 10,000-meter events. However, rather than cashing in on rich endorsement deals or creating branded speed-skating academies or the like, Heiden decided to pursue his long-held dream of going back to medical school and becoming an orthopedic surgeon, a position he has enjoyed to this day. Dr. Heiden remains a championship performer, just in a different discipline.

An altogether different means to build a personal legacy, one that is frequently underappreciated, is to be a "champion" parent. Trite as it may sound, leading children by example and inspiring them to contribute to the world as active and healthy participants in society is a legacy that is available to everyone with children of their own, nieces or nephews, or students in school. On a highly personal level, I have found creative ways to apply the lessons from The Dynamic Path to my own parenting, such as helping my children set goals, deal with disappointments, and ascertain what's truly important to them.

One can also leave a legacy without following The Dynamic Path or necessarily becoming a moral or spiritual leader. Think about the legacies left by the Wright brothers, Thomas Edison, Vincent Van Gogh, Mozart, and Louis Pasteur. Creators, such as inventors, artists, or scientists, possess the perhaps unique ability to impact the world in major and positive ways while working relatively independently. Their achievements share many of the same factors that drive The Dynamic Path. However, their accomplishments are in selected endeavors where the very achievement itself serves to inspire and change the world. Their individual work *is* their legacy.

If The Dynamic Path is for you, it generally starts with a decision.

Dynamic Moment I

Deciding to Become a Champion

Sometimes it comes early in life. For Billie Jean King, it was at 5 or 6 years old, when she told her mother that she would be *the best* in something one day. By the time she was 12, she knew exactly what it would be.

"Billie Jean, what are you going to do with your life?" her pastor asked her one day. She replied, "Reverend, I'm going to be the best tennis player in the world."

When she told her mother the same thing on the way home from the local tennis courts one day, her mom's reaction was predictable: "*That's very nice, Billie Jean.*" Billie Jean was undeterred. Growing up in the 1950s, she was part of a struggling middle-class family, and her parents had well-defined roles. Her dad made the money and her mom took care of the home, which allowed her to drive Billie Jean all over Southern California to play the best tennis players in the region. Not only did her natural talent and competitive drive enable her to win on the court, her personal dynamism caused her to have an important influence on other players. Even kids who were years older than her came to Billie Jean for advice and counsel. Some time later, Billie Jean recounts, "I had this epiphany, that if God was going to give me these gifts, I was not only going to become the world's best player, but I would do everything in my power to make this world a better place."

So began Billie Jean's quest to conquer tennis and to change the world.

Billie Jean King is justifiably proud of her athletic achievements, but she is most fulfilled by her efforts to create equal rights for women in sports and more broadly in society. Her historic win in 1973 over Bobby Riggs in the "Battle of the Sexes" is a symbolic turning point in the role of women in society. Her pioneering work on the legislation that became Title IX put governmental policy squarely behind equal access and resources for women. The millions of girl athletes in the United States and around the world are a major part of Billie Jean's legacy. In 1972, the first year of Title IX, under 300,000 girls participated in high school sports nationwide, just 7 percent of the total number of high school athletes. Today the number is approximately 3,500,000—roughly half of the 7.2 million students who participate in high school sports. Many sports, such as swimming and diving, volleyball, water polo, and tennis, now have greater numbers of girl participants than boys, and others, such as soccer and lacrosse, are almost even. Overall, the number of girls playing organized sports continues to grow.

In 1967, Billie Jean King was selected as "Outstanding Female Athlete of the World." In 1972, she was named *Sports Illustrated* magazine's "Sportsperson of the Year," the first woman to be so honored. For more than 20 years, from the time she was first ranked in the top 10 at age 17, until she retired from active playing in 1984, King was a dominant force in the world of tennis. As a player, she won a record 20 Wimbledon titles, 13 US Open titles, the French Open, the Australian Open, and 29 Virginia Slims singles titles. She was ranked number one in the world seven times between 1966 and 1974. She was also the first woman athlete to earn more than $100,000 in a single year, a feat recognized by a telephone call from President Richard Nixon.

"As great a champion as Billie Jean was," says fellow tennis legend Chris Evert, "I don't even think about what she did on the court as much as how she had the vision to look ahead and see how far she could take not only women's tennis, but women's sports." King's energy and leadership turned women's tennis into a major professional sport, with ramifications far beyond the confines of the court. "As player, promoter, and innovator, she has done more to advance the cause of women's sports than any man or woman, before or since," intoned the announcer in welcoming her to Wimbledon's Centre Court in 2005. Years earlier, outraged at the disparity between men's and women's prize money at major tournaments, King spearheaded the drive for equal compensation and equal treatment of women (only recently did Wimbledon, the last holdout among the majors, award equal prize money to women). She helped establish the Virginia Slims professional tennis tour for women in 1970, and she founded the Women's Tennis Association. King became the first woman commissioner in professional sports history, and in 1989, she became the chief executive officer of World Team Tennis.

Billie Jean King transcended her own achievements, and in doing so, she cleared the way for others. She launched the Women's Sports Foundation, which has educated thousands of girls, mothers, fathers, coaches, and administrators on the value of females participating in sports activities. The foundation has granted millions of dollars in scholarships and training to aspiring women athletes and lobbied governments and educational institutions for equal opportunities for women in sports. Donna Lopiano, CEO of the Women's Sports Foundation, says it best: "Billie Jean King made Title IX real. She lifted the heads and hearts of women at a critical time in history."

The ultimate recognition of her pioneering efforts to change tennis and launch the drive for gender equality in sports and in society was bestowed upon her on August 28, 2006. On the opening night of the 2006 US Open, the United States Tennis Association performed a moving ceremony that renamed the USTA National Tennis Center—the world's largest public tennis facility and home of the US Open—the USTA Billie Jean King National Tennis Center. Frank Deford, co-author of Billie Jean King's autobiography, put this honor in context. "She and Jackie

Robinson are the two figures in sports that stand out in our culture. She should be [so] honored for what she did. She did a lot."

BUILDING ON KING'S WORK

King's example has paved the way for other great achievers. One need not go back to the 1970s for such examples. By the age of 29, Mia Hamm was the world's best-known female soccer player and one of the most talked about names in athletics, male or female. An Olympic gold medalist, a World Cup champion, and a three-time all-American collegiate star, she graced the cover of *Sports Illustrated* and captured the public's attention. Like King, Hamm is not likely to be remembered only for her athletic accolades. Hamm fueled the popularity of women's soccer as a phenomenal player and then went on to help start the Women's United Soccer Association (WUSA), America's first professional women's soccer league.

Hamm has leveraged her popularity to inspire thousands of young girls to take up competitive sports. She started the Mia Hamm Foundation, dedicated to helping with bone marrow research and to helping women's sports programs progress. Her inspiration for the foundation was her adoptive brother and original athletic inspiration, Garrett, who died of a bone marrow disease shortly after her gold-medal win at the 1996 Olympics.

How good a player was Hamm? At the age of 15, Hamm became the youngest member of the US National Soccer Team. At 17, she went to the University of North Carolina at Chapel Hill, a powerhouse in women's soccer, and became a four-time member of the NCAA champion UNC team, completing her collegiate career as the conference's all-time top scorer in goals (103), assists (72), and points (278). She had her UNC number (19) retired in 1994. With Hamm as the star, the US National Soccer Team went on to win World Cup Championships in 1991 and

1999, capture gold medals at the 1996 Atlanta Olympics and the 1998 Goodwill Games, and win the silver medal at the Sydney Olympics in 2000. She completed her 17-year career at age 32 with a gold medal at the 2004 Olympics, having scored a world-record 153 career goals. Phil Knight, founder and chairman of Nike and an expert on sports champions, said, "I think we've had just three athletes who played at a level that added a new dimension to their sports. That's been Michael Jordan in basketball, Tiger Woods in golf, and Mia Hamm in women's soccer." In April 1999, Nike named the largest building on its corporate campus after Mia.

It is curious to ponder whether there would have even been a "Mia Hamm" if there had never been a "Billie Jean King." Hamm was born in 1972, the same year as the enactment of Title IX.

"What Billie Jean did in fighting for Title IX, they were thinking about people like me," Hamm says. "Today, I feel a personal responsibility to build on her important work to create future opportunities for young girls."

THE CHART ON THE WALL

Grant Hackett was 14 years old when he put himself on the course to become perhaps the greatest distance swimmer in the history of the sport. The captain of the Australian national swim team, Hackett won the men's 1,500-meter freestyle gold medal at both the 2000 Olympics in Sydney and the 2004 Olympics in Athens. He is the fastest swimmer of all time at the 1,500 meters and 800 meters and second fastest at the 400 meters.

The teenage Hackett had the simple idea to pin up a chart on his bedroom wall in his Queensland, Australia, home. The chart showed the best times that his idol, Kieren Perkins, had reached when he was a 14-, 15-, 16-, 17-, and 18-year-old swimmer. Perkins, 7 years Hackett's senior, was also an Australian, and, at that time, the world's best 1,500-meter freestyler, holding both an Olympic gold medal and the world record. The chart gave Hackett a concrete method to set his goals and to track his progress. "Soon I came up with the idea that I'd just try and do the same times that he did when he was at my same age. So I put the times up on the wall for the 200-, 400-, 800-, and 1,500-meter free-styles because I knew I wanted to do all those events."

How well did it work? "I've obviously bettered him for about 80 or 90 percent of his times," Hackett adds. "It was very important to define my goals, because they determined how hard I had to train in order to achieve them." The times on the charts were motivating. They focused Hackett's training and racing efforts and allowed him to track his prog-ress. "Every time I finished swimming, I could go back and see exactly where I was. I was then able to determine what I had to do to improve my times in training in order to achieve those times in my races over the next season. I also figured out that if I didn't meet the goals in one par-ticular event during one year, I could try to make them the next year."

Setting measurable goals is an essential step. But some people avoid being specific because they don't want to expose themselves to the risk or fear of failing. "While quantifying particular goals makes them easier to achieve," Hackett says, "you need to understand that being so specific does also put pressure on yourself. You need to be able to work with the demands of putting that sort of commitment on your shoulders. You've got to be able to use goal setting, work with it, and let it enhance, rather than be detrimental to, your performance."

Applying Hackett's goal-setting approach to a career in business is a subtle affair. Yes, it is important to have short-term, quantifiable goals. Effective short-term goal setting involves achieving committed-to results during the current quarter or year, the development of an important new skill this month, or the successful completion of a high-priority project within the agreed-upon time frame. But it's also essential to focus on longer-term career management, which is more like captaining a sailboat than ticking off tasks on a to-do list. The most successful professionals keep their eyes on the horizon—their long-term goals—while simultaneously navigating the conditions immediately in front of them. In my earlier research on extraordinary careers, the highest-performing executives were significantly more likely to focus on long-term goals in addition to short-term objectives, while less successful employees focused principally on the short term. Setting sound long-term professional goals, however, is distinct from taking it too far and trying to micromanage your career. In the latter case, some are so obsessed with one specific goal, such as becoming a CEO, that when they finally get there, often at the expense of other important dimensions of their lives, their feelings of emptiness or unhappiness make them realize that this was the wrong goal to have set in the first place.

DOESN'T EVERYONE WANT TO BE THE BEST?

The green flag of Les Palmiers beach club was fluttering in the warm seaside breeze in August 1984. Around me were rows and rows of bronzed bikini- and mono-kini-clad sunbathers splayed out on beach mattresses at the posh St. Tropez resort. Some were reading *Paris-Match* or *Les Echoes,* while others were sleeping, smoking Gaulois, or sipping cocktails with paper umbrellas. A few were fortunate enough to have music courtesy of their then brand-new Sony Walkmans. My best buddies, Cliff, Barry, Doug, and Etienne, with whom I was summering, fell right into the oiled-up, hedonistic rhythm of the place. But I had a slightly different agenda.

While they were tanning and partying, I was enjoying myself in a different way. In preparation for going to business school the following month, I was reading Paul Johnson's *Modern Times: A History of the Modern World*, taking quizzes in *The Essentials of Accounting* workbook, and wielding my highlighter across Graham and Dodd's *Securities Analysis*. For lighter fare, I was enjoying Peters and Waterman's new bestseller, *In Search of Excellence*. Although I'm sure I sound like a total nerd, I was in heaven. My view was then—and remains today—that vacations are the best time to learn, improve, and develop. I distinctly remember a conversation with Barry, one of my best friends since third grade.

"Don't you have a profound desire to be the best?" I asked him on the beach that day. He looked at me, paused, and then said with a Cheshire cat grin, "To be honest, that's really not what I'm thinking about, especially around here."

I had thought that the desire to be the best, to become a champion, was hardwired into everyone. But that clearly is not the case. That desire, which, for those who have it, is more like a primal need, turns out to be just one of many different naturally endowed attributes from nature's Chinese menu of possibilities. For me, this driving motivation was well articulated in Buckingham and Clifton's seminal work, *Now, Discover Your Strengths*. "Talents not only have an 'I can't help it' quality to them," they wrote, "but also an 'it feels good' quality." When I read this book some 17 years after our St. Tropez adventure, it brought clarity to that sun-struck conversation.

MY STRENGTHS

Most people have a few dominant themes that determine what they are good at, what they enjoy doing, and as a consequence, how they should organize their lives. Buckingham and Clifton memorably coined 34 different themes to describe the combination of attributes and attitudes that combine to make up different people.[1] Their list ranges from "Developer" and "Relator" to "Maximizer" and "Ideation." The two themes

[1] The theme names of the Clifton StrengthsFinder are trademarks of the Gallup Organization.

that clearly describe me are "Achiever" and "Significance." Not to put myself in the company of Billie Jean King or Grant Hackett, but I suspect that both they and many other champions (including some readers of this book) share these same two attributes.

Here's a description of Achiever:

> *Your Achiever theme helps explain your drive. Achiever describes a constant need for achievement. You feel as if every day starts at zero. By the end of the day you must achieve something tangible in order to feel good about yourself. And by "every day" you mean every single day— workdays, weekends, vacation. You have an internal fire burning inside you. It pushes you to do more, to achieve more. After each accomplishment is reached, the fire dwindles for a moment, but very soon it rekindles itself, forcing you toward the next accomplishment. It is the power supply that causes you to set the pace and define the levels of productivity for you and your group.*

When I read this, I thought, "Wow, this finally explains it." No wonder I was happy only when doing something "productive" like reading, studying language, or training for a triathlon. It also explained why my friends thought I was nuts (and they may not have been wrong). But when one Achiever finds another, it is as if two long-lost siblings have come together. So *this* is where my fire comes from.

What about how I want to be viewed among my peers and in the world at large? The "Significance" theme explains that.

> *You want to be very significant in the eyes of other people. In the truest sense of the word you want to be recognized. You want to be heard. You want to stand out. You want to be known. You feel a need to be admired as credible,*

professional, and successful. Likewise, you want to associate with others who are credible, professional, and successful. And if they aren't, you will push them to achieve until they are. Or you will move on. An independent spirit, you want your work to be a way of life rather than a job, and in that work you want to be given free rein, the leeway to do things your way. Your yearnings feel intense to you, and you honor those yearnings. And so your life is filled with goals, achievements, or qualifications that you crave. Whatever your focus, your Significance theme will keep pulling you upward, away from the mediocre toward the exceptional. It is the theme that keeps you reaching.

This description is uncannily accurate as well. When I consider what these two themes mean to me and how they interrelate, they help explain the way I perceive my life and career, even the drive to write this book. I thrive on the sense of accomplishment every time I win and then complete an important executive search engagement or finish an interview or writing an article or book section, and on having an endless source of material to dig into as soon as the rest of my responsibilities have been dispatched. I readily admit that I also want to be known as a thought leader, and through my work and writing, to spend time with and become associated with the most successful leaders in business, sports, and other walks of life. Just as the Achiever and Significance themes pertain to me and describe what traits I favor to pursue my personal goals and interests, there are many different attributes (34 additional ones, per Buckingham and Clifton) that others can and do apply. The key is to be studious in understanding your natural capabilities, sufficiently dedicated to turn these talents into strengths, and thoughtful enough to apply these strengths to whatever you do to realize your greatest potential.

✦

Jerry Green—
Pro Football Hall of Famer and My Uncle

On August 6, 2005, at the induction ceremony for the Pro Football Hall of Fame in Canton, Ohio, Jerry Green stepped up to the podium to begin his acceptance speech before a large crowd.

"I've always been a storyteller," he said. "So I thought it would be appropriate to tell you a story. Once upon a time there was a boy who wanted to be a professional athlete, like today's inductees, Dan Marino and Steve Young. The rude awakening came at age 16, however, when he realized that he couldn't throw a pass 10 yards, couldn't kick a football, and couldn't hit a curve ball. So the boy did the next best thing. He became a sportswriter."

Although a low-key person, Jerry is a renowned figure in the sports-crazed city of Detroit, Michigan. He has been the sports columnist for one of the city's two leading papers, the *Detroit News,* as well as a regular contributor to *Sports Illustrated* and *The Sporting News.* Among his many sports journalism achievements, the most notable was the fact that as of 2007, he was one of only five journalists alive who had covered every one of the 41 Super Bowl games ever played. Journalists are inducted into the Pro Football Hall of Fame each year, one from print journalism and one from radio and television broadcasting. Jerry won the Dick McCann Memorial Award, which was started in 1969, for long and distinguished print reporting in football.

I never realized it, but perhaps this book is one aspect of Jerry Green's legacy. Growing up, I lived 800 miles away and was not a big Detroit fan, but I always felt a special bond to Uncle Jerry. The older brother of my mother, he was central to some stories that were a part of family lore growing up. The most memorable was when Uncle Jerry was on the junior high school football team. It was game day and he was out sick. Even though he was a third stringer and had never seen game action, he did not want to lose his place on the roster by being absent. So he convinced his younger sister, who happened to be a very good athlete, to go onto the sidelines and take his place wearing his uniform and keeping the helmet on her head. "What if you were told to go in?" we used to delight in asking Mom. "I would have gone in and played," she always boasted with a smile.

One day in 1970, Uncle Jerry came to our home and gave my brother Jeff, sister Nancy, and me each a signed copy of his new book, *Year of the Tiger: The Diary of Detroit's World Champions*, celebrating the Tigers' stunning seven-game World Series victory over the St. Louis Cardinals. I can still remember the special feeling of holding that book in my hands, seeing his picture on the back flap, and reading his handwritten personalized dedication.

Jerry was born in 1928, the son of my maternal grandparents, Frank and Sylvia Green. He grew up in Great Neck, New York, listening to the Giants and Yankees on the radio, and saw his first Giants game at the Polo Grounds in 1936 as an 8-year-old. He saw Lou Gehrig play his final game at Yankee Stadium. He loved playing baseball and football but realized at a young age that he had neither the size nor the talent to pursue either as a career. Jerry began reading the sports pages at an early age, so when it came time to choose a career direction, he combined his two interests—sports and journalism. After graduating from Brown University in 1950, he received his master's degree in journalism from Boston College and started his career as a copyboy for the *New York Journal-American* in the fall of 1952. He moved to Detroit to accept a job with the Associated Press in 1956. In 1963, he was hired by the *Detroit News*, and for 41 years, he became the paper's sports identity. He covered Michigan football, was the Lions beat writer and attended World Series; Stanley Cup Finals; NBA Finals; Wimbledon; the British Open and the US golf and tennis Opens; the Masters and other PGA events; NCAA basketball tournaments; the Rose, Sugar, Orange, Cotton, and Fiesta Bowls; NFL play-offs; and the Indy 500, among many, many more.

For years, I have asked anyone I meet from Detroit if they know Jerry Green. If they have even a passing interest in sports, the answer is invariably yes. The quality of his writing, the relationships he built with the players and coaches, and the breadth and longevity of his coverage have demonstrated the significance and impact of his work for others.

MAKE A DECISION

Okay, not everyone needs or even wants to become the best. But if you do, it starts with an instinct and moves quickly to a decision. In the pages that follow, I address the actions that everyone must take to become a champion and the *decisions* that you must make in your life, e.g., to be committed, to be mentally tough, etc., if you want to follow this path. The essence of the dynamic moment is about understanding the challenges that are in front of you and deciding that the outcome is worth your effort.

For example, for the past 3 years, I have been working closely with a senior executive of a major global media and information company; let's call him David. At the time I met him, the company's chief executive saw the enormous potential resident in David, who was by far the youngest of the top five executives in the company. Despite his high position, there were serious gaps in his experience and skill set that would hold him back from further advancement. Even though I am not an "executive coach" armed with a PhD, the CEO and the company's board thought I was best positioned to work with David because of my experience assessing top executives as CEO candidates.

Here's where David had to make a decision. After 11 years of steadily working his way up the company ladder, did he want to embrace the process and use it to get closer to his long-term business leadership aspirations? Or would he treat it as a perfunctory exercise and just try to get through it?

Of course, he embraced it (otherwise it wouldn't have made for a particularly good example). In the first months of the consulting assignment, we created a set of concrete short-term goals that supported the more general long-term aspiration of helping the company attain worldwide leadership in its media markets. His most important gap was an imbalance between superior strategy and mergers and acquisition skills on one hand and limited operating expertise on the other. The near-term priorities that we developed were centered on instituting an organized management process for his division that would create a rhythm of individual and group meetings and supporting management reports. Over the subsequent two quarters, it became evident to his management team and to the CEO that David was becoming "an operator." The division's results also thrived. The next set of goals was to become a "collector" of good questions and rely more on an ask-don't-tell management style. Like an expert litigator, he became highly skilled in the use of increasingly penetrating questions to get to the heart of important business and organizational issues. The final priority for the first year was to make some difficult personnel decisions. One resulted in firing a talented and long-serving, but organizationally toxic, senior executive. When David finally made this tough call, the positive energy released across the division was palpable, and it far outweighed the resulting loss of productivity and institutional memory.

Eighteen months into the development program, David's internal reputation had been transformed. He had become known as the executive who worked most effectively with his team and as the best operating manager in the company's senior leadership team. David was rewarded by the CEO and the board with the appointment to chief operating officer of the company. Had this promotion been made without him having developed new operating skills, he would likely have been met with resentment as the golden boy, the CEO's pet. But in fact it was seen as fitting, logical, and well deserved. Now, a year and a half later, after a valedictory cover story in a major business publication and his election to a prestigious corporate board, David's external reputation has followed suit. Culminating his ascension as a business leader, he was recently tapped by his board as the designated CEO successor of the company.

Sometimes the decision hits you like a bolt of lightning, as it did for Billie Jean King. Other times it is a gradual process that at some point culminates in deciding to set an ambitious goal, as it did for David. Personally, I'm in the bolt-of-lightning camp. I can remember specific turning-point moments in my life when it literally struck me that I wanted to get a summer job in Paris, go to Harvard Business School, marry a woman named Gail whom I had just met a few hours before, join Spencer Stuart, write a book, become a leader in the executive recruiting field, and become a nationally ranked tennis player (this last goal is still very far away . . . but I'm working on it).

Chances are that the decisions that constitute a dynamic moment will coincide with a point in your life when you reach a crossroads. Essentially, there is a perilous moment when, in order to continue growing and developing, change becomes essential. If you just keep doing what you have been doing that got you to that point, your skills and relevance will inevitably begin to deteriorate. It brings to mind the gas station attendant in the middle of nowhere giving directions to the befuddled out-of-towner, "You can't get there from here," he twangs.

Well, making your decision will help you get there from here. The decision that constitutes a dynamic moment needs to be a parfait composed of one part dreams and two parts reality. The dreams will benefit from ambitious goal setting and a deep belief in your cause and in yourself. The reality demands an unwavering level of commitment, an ability to control distractions, and realistic self-assessment.

Let's take a look at each in turn.

THE POWER OF DREAMS AND GOALS

"YOU'VE GOT TO HAVE DREAMS AND HOPES, AND YOU CAN'T
LET ANYBODY TAKE THEM AWAY FROM YOU. I REMEMBER WHEN
I WAS 13, MY FIRST COACH SAYING, 'YOU'RE TOO SMALL. YOU'RE
5 FEET 2 INCHES. YOU BARELY WEIGH 100 POUNDS. YOU CAN'T
POSSIBLY HOPE TO DO WHAT YOU WANT TO DO.' AND I WENT
AND DID IT."

—DONNA DE VARONA
United States swimming, two Olympic gold medals, 1964 Tokyo

Becoming a champion is grounded in trusting that your aspirations merit significance and that you have the capacity and potential to reach those goals. You must believe that you are investing your life in something worthwhile and that you have a legitimate chance of making it happen. And then you need to make it real; you need to translate your aspirations and faith in what you are doing into more specific goals. Like compound interest that allows modest sums to grow into millions over time, expansive goals can be reached by setting and achieving incremental and interim goals. This phenomenon was articulated in one way or another by every single athlete, coach, and leader that I interviewed for this book. It is, moreover, common practice among the most successful performers in business, finance, politics, science, medicine, and the arts.

Take the case of one of the greatest champions in Olympic history. Eric Heiden attained the singular achievement of winning five gold medals in the 1980 Lake Placid Olympics. Of course he had extraordinary talent, lung capacity, power, grace, and all the other dimensions necessary to succeed. But he channeled these strengths through his goal-setting process to set and keep him on the path toward being the best speed skater in history.

Heiden was raised in Madison, Wisconsin. Growing up, he was exposed to a range of different sports, and he was a strong hockey player.

Heiden and a number of his teammates were recruited into speed skating by the local Madison Speed Skating Club to participate in city races. While speed skating was popular in his hometown, the numbers were still small. The club had only about 25 people skating, but it was enough to create the community and motivating environment that stoked him. He gravitated toward speed skating based on his strong early results. "I think success kind of breeds more success," Heiden says. "Also, I had a coach who showed up in Madison to become the coach for our local speed skating team who was very motivating. In fact, he stayed with me all the way and was my coach during the Olympics."

Heiden says that by age 14, he wanted to be in the Olympics. "That was an ambitious goal, for sure, but I had smaller goals set along the way that would give me a sense of accomplishment on a daily and monthly level." For example, he continued, "in some instances, one goal was just to know that at the end of a day, I had trained literally as hard as I could. Doing that provided me with a satisfying sense of accomplishment on a daily level." This was no idle goal. Heiden is said to have punished himself so severely in his workouts that other skaters could not stay on the ice with him. "Another goal was to achieve a personal best time for a particular distance," Heiden says. "Then I had set the goal of winning a championship the following winter. The subsequent goal was getting on the national team. From there, it wasn't too much of a stretch to set the goal of making the Olympic team. Finally, I established the goal of winning the World Championships and the Olympics. These were certainly grand goals. Even if I might not have ever really expected to make them, it was always nice to set these kinds of challenges out in front of me."

After his Olympic glory, Heiden said that the Madison Speed Skating Club rose to its peak level of popularity. The number of skaters ballooned tenfold—to 250 skaters. Today, it's settled back to about 50 people—still double the level of when he started.

The greatest sports champions and business leaders are also the best goal setters. For ambitious people determined to make steady progress against their most significant aspirations, goal setting is an essential cornerstone in the process.

BELIEF

"IT TAKES TALENT, DISCIPLINE, A VERY STRONG WORK ETHIC, AND A LOVE FOR YOUR SPORT TO BE AN OLYMPIC CHAMPION. BUT THAT'S ONLY 50 PERCENT OF IT. I WOULDN'T HAVE BECOME AN OLYMPIC CHAMPION WITHOUT THE OTHER 50 PERCENT THAT MY COACH, BELA KAROLYI, GAVE ME. HE MADE ME BELIEVE THE UNBELIEVABLE, THAT I COULD BE OLYMPIC CHAMPION."
—**MARY LOU RETTON**
United States gymnastics, Olympic gold, silver, and bronze medalist, 1984 Los Angeles

Belief in your mission, belief in yourself, and belief in your teammates and colleagues: these are the elements of support that help turn aspirations into accomplishments and goals into distant memories. When you believe in others with whom you are pursuing your goals—whether a coach, a teammate, a partner, or a manager—and when you know that these people also believe in you, your confidence level will be enhanced. Everyone needs the support and stimulation of others to excel. It is important to have at least one person—a coach, a spouse, or a mentor of some sort—who genuinely believes in you, makes you feel valued, and supports your goals.

Have you ever been on a high-performing team or worked in an extraordinary organization, one with a tradition of excellence and winning results? If you have, you know that this is a result of a group of talented people who share an unwavering commitment to success, who genuinely believe they can achieve it, and who work well together with a strong sense of ownership in pursuing it. Although less than half of working Americans report that they are satisfied with their jobs (down from 61 percent 20 years ago), according to The Conference Board, there are certain organizations where people are continually challenged and motivated. Goldman Sachs, McKinsey & Company, General Electric, Starbucks, and more recently Google are the kinds of winning institutions where members share the self-confidence and feelings of propriety that allow everyone to believe that they have a meaningful role to play in the organization's success. Sean Fitzpatrick, captain of arguably the greatest sports franchise in history, the New Zealand All Blacks rugby team, knows what it feels like to be a part of such a team. "When a team member puts on the All Blacks jersey," Fitzpatrick says, "he knows that we can win, that we must win. Winning as an All Black is not about the individual, or even about today's team. Each player feels part of an unbroken tradition going back over a century. The entire nation of four million New Zealanders takes national pride and identity in our result."

Now that sentiment is certainly one to point to.

COMMITMENT

"IT'S 5:30 P.M. AND IT'S SNOWY. IT'S CHRISTMAS EVE, BUT JUST THINK—NOBODY WILL BE AT THE RINK AND YOU CAN TRAIN FOR 5 HOURS STRAIGHT. AND IT WILL ALL PAY OFF SOMEDAY."
—CAROL HEISS
United States figure skating, Olympic silver medalist, 1956 Cortina;
gold medalist, 1960 Squaw Valley

There is nothing more important in turning your goals and aspirations into reality than hard work and commitment. In the next chapter, we'll explore this more deeply. For now, recognize that the base ingredient for developing the mental, physical, and technical skills you need to achieve your goals is relentless commitment. While some people may be graced with a slightly larger intrinsic dosage of work ethic and the ability to dedicate themselves, commitment is really a conscious choice. It starts with an acknowledgment of its importance. It is followed by the decision to commit yourself. Then, similar to developing any skill, your commitment abilities will improve through the continuous practice of applying yourself. To truly excel, you must have a high degree of self-discipline, a passion for what you are doing, and a consistent focus on self-improvement.

Pete Dawkins, the Heisman Trophy football player for West Point, Rhodes Scholar, and youngest brigadier general in US Army history, has seen extraordinary performers in a wide range of different fields over the course of his distinguished career. He has known leaders from science, academia, business, the arts, music, the military, politics, and sports. He said that the most common thread about excellence across all of these disciplines is that the best performers are more committed and work harder than anyone else. "It's kind of an aw-shucks conclusion," Dawkins says, "but Yo-Yo Ma, who I think is generally considered to be the best cellist in the world, performs more concerts, travels more, works harder at his craft than any other cellist. Just go down the line and you'll see that the people who are the very best in the world not only have a passion and a genius for what they do, but they work the hardest."

DISTRACTION CONTROL

"ON PURPOSE, MY COACH PLACED THE SHOOTING STAND RIGHT IN AN ANTHILL. WHEN I SHOT FROM THIS STAND ON HOT SUMMER DAYS, MY LEGS WERE IMMEDIATELY COVERED WITH ANTS. THIS WAS VERY DISTURBING, ESPECIALLY WHEN THEY REACHED MY FACE."

—MAGNAR SOLBERG
Norway biathlon, Olympic gold medalist, 1972 Sapporo and 1968 Grenoble

You don't have to be eaten alive by red ants while training; there are other creative ways to achieve the mental toughness you need to become a champion. Aimee Kimball, PhD, a leading sports psychologist, described the "prescription" that she developed for the UCLA softball team that was having trouble letting go and regaining a positive focus after suffering a bad inning. "They actually put a fake toilet in their dugout," she said, "and after every inning, whether it was good or bad, they'd come in and flush the toilet. The image was flushing that inning away." Whether the inning was bad or good, the important thing was that they would let go of the past and focus on what they could control. This kind of stunt works, according to Dr. Kimball, because to regain your focus and rid yourself of recurring negative thoughts, you actually need to replace them with something else. "If you don't have something else to focus on, the distracting thoughts will keep coming back," she says.

Regaining focus and quickly reclaiming a positive state of mind is central to overcoming distractions and getting back into the zone. As another technique to help bring this about, Dr. Kimball works with her athletes to come up with a meaningful word to serve as a prompt. Like a Pavlovian signal, articulating the trigger word reminds athletes to concentrate on what they can control—their focus—and let the other things go. One of her favorites was from a hockey player she worked with whose word was *catalyst*. Dr. Kimball said, "Every time he crossed over the boards he would say 'catalyst,' and that would remind him that he wanted to be the person on the ice that got things started and really made things happen." In another case, she coached a baseball team's designated hitter to recover from a severe batting slump. "He had all these worries about letting his team down," Dr. Kimball said, "and negative thoughts about striking out beset him each time he came up to bat." She asked the player what he wanted to be thinking about when at the plate, and he said, "I just want to make good, solid contact with the ball. That's all." So Dr. Kimball prescribed his trigger word, *contact*. "He actually took a baseball, wrote the word 'contact' on it, and carried it around with him," she said. "Every time he saw the baseball he would see that word. Eventually when he was up at bat he was able to clear everything else out of his mind with just that word in his head."

SELF-ASSESSMENT

"MY MOM TAUGHT ME THAT YOU SHOULD LEARN MORE FROM EVERY MATCH YOU LOSE THAN EVERY MATCH YOU WIN. SO I STARTED ANALYZING EVERY MATCH, IMMEDIATELY SITTING DOWN TO THINK ABOUT IT AND DO AN HONEST EVALUATION OF WHAT HAPPENED OUT THERE. IF ANYTHING HAD TO DO WITH ANY WEAKNESSES THAT I HAD, I WOULD THEN GO ON TO WORK OUT THOSE WEAKNESSES."
—JOHN NEWCOMBE
Australia, US Open and Wimbledon tennis champion

"COMPLACENCY IS A SUCCESSFUL ATHLETE'S GREATEST PSYCHOLOGICAL ENEMY. ONCE YOU START TAKING YOUR VICTORIES FOR GRANTED, SOMEONE WILL PUT AN END TO YOUR WINNING STREAK. YOU MUST CONSTANTLY FIND AREAS TO IMPROVE."
—STEVEN REDGRAVE
Great Britain rowing, five-time Olympic gold medalist: 1984 Los Angeles, 1988 Seoul, 1992 Barcelona, 1996 Atlanta, 2000 Sydney

A final thing that will help set you on the path to achieving excellence and becoming a champion in sports and a star performer in business is the process of critically assessing yourself and acting on the lessons learned. This will both reinforce those things that you do or have done well and target areas for improvement. After each competition or important presentation or assignment at work, you should evaluate your overall performance. How did you do at the critical portions of the effort? How was your mental state? Did it reinforce your capabilities or cause anxiety that sapped energy from your effort? Through experience, the best performers have developed individualized ways to assess themselves and take corrective action that works for them. Here is one such approach.

In 1986, I was a first-year associate at the investment bank Goldman Sachs. One evening I found myself on the 29th floor of the firm's 85 Broad Street, New York, headquarters and ran into the chief of the firm's equities division, a legend in the business named Richard Menschel. He sat me down in his glass-walled office and told me what he said was his single best piece of advice. "At the end of each week, spend a few minutes reviewing all the things that you did that went well and the things that did not work. Then commit, each week, to make one concrete change to improve the things that didn't work. Develop this as a habit," he said, "and you will be amazed at its power and impact." What he was saying was that making single improvements one after the other will build upon itself and over time have an extraordinary impact on performance.

That piece of advice came to me more than 20 years ago. I sometimes think about what I could have achieved if I had followed it in a more disciplined and systematic way.

As important as it is to make the decisions and set the goals that constitute the first dynamic moment, they are only the launching point. To unleash your talents, dedicate yourself, and develop the mental toughness to actually become a champion in sports or business—the very best you can be—you need to move into action. Let's now turn to those next stages of *The Dynamic Path* and delve into the body and then the mind of a champion.

CHAPTER 4

The Body of a Champion

When he was 10 years old, he ran 18 miles home from school cross-country. He had never high-jumped before, but one day as a college student, he watched the track team's jumpers in practice. When the bar was set at 5 feet 9 inches, he stepped up and asked if he could try. No one on the team could clear that height, and no one expected the young man in overalls and street shoes to be able to do so either. But jump he did, and Jim Thorpe cleared the bar with ease and grace. He was also an accomplished tennis player, golfer, rower, bowler, and gymnast, and he went on to become an Olympic champion and world-record holder in the decathlon. If all that was not enough, he also had championship careers in Major League Baseball and professional football, going to the World Series and the League Championship, respectively.

Perhaps no one has ever been endowed with such extraordinary natural athletic talents as Jim Thorpe. So great was he that in 1999, Congress passed a resolution naming Thorpe "America's Athlete of the 20th Century."

NATURALLY ENDOWED TALENT

I remember the first time I saw John McEnroe play tennis. It was in 1972 at the Port Washington Tennis Academy in Long Island, New York. I was 12 years old and McEnroe was 13. At that time, Port Washington, under the iron-fisted direction of former Australia Davis Cup captain Harry Hopman, was the epicenter of the junior tennis scene in the United States. McEnroe, playing on the middle court in front of the lounge, wasn't particularly tall or even terribly athletic looking. But I quickly became mesmerized by his control of his wooden Wilson Jack Kramer Pro Staff racquet. He wielded it with such confidence and authority. I longed to be able to control the ball the way he did, guiding his top-spin serve with a precision I could never match and a pace I could never muster. His touch, spin, control, and sheer confidence all added up to a guy who seemed to be born for the court. He was natural talent personified.

If only . . .

If only I had been endowed with such natural talent, then I could have become a champion too. Right?

Perhaps.

The question rages not only in sports, where Tiger Woods is held up as exhibit A, having hit his first hole-in-one at age 6; but also in music, where child prodigies have amazed audiences since Wolfgang Amadeus Mozart played for the Bavarian elector and the Austrian empress after proving himself as a composer at the age of 5; in chess, where Bobby Fischer became a grandmaster at age 16; among inventors, where Thomas Edison is considered the patron saint, making one of his first inventions, the "automatic repeater" at age 16; and even in business. Warren Buffett once told *Fortune* magazine that he was "wired at birth to allocate capital." Many take it as a given that exceptional individuals, whose performance in any discipline is vastly superior to that of the rest of the population, have capabilities and characteristics that are innate and genetically transmitted.

By this reasoning, you either have the gift, or you don't.

Not so fast. Natural talent isn't actually the most important ingredient in greatness, according to K. Anders Ericsson, PhD, a renowned professor of human achievement at Florida State University. The notion that excelling is a consequence of possessing innate abilities is simply not supported by evidence, according to Dr. Ericsson's research. He has found that expert performers are distinguished *not* by their heritable characteristics, but rather by their ability to continue improving for years, even decades, until they become great. Expert performance is the end result of individuals' prolonged efforts to improve through a regimen of deliberate, targeted activities specifically designed to optimize improvement. Differences among performers, even among the most elite, are a function of the amount and duration of deliberate practice that they undertake. This holds true, according to Dr. Ericsson, across the fields of sports, music, and chess, in which performance is relatively easy to measure and track over time. Many characteristics once believed to reflect innate talent are actually the result of intense practice for a minimum of 10 years. So strong is the finding that it takes at least a decade of dedicated work, deliberate practice, and development to become elite that performance experts call it the 10-year rule.

But excellence can't be the result of hard work and directed practice alone. Natural talent must be inherent in those who become great champions. This interplay between naturally endowed qualities in both body and mind and dedication, sheer effort, and mental strengths is the core of this chapter and the next.

CARMICHAEL & COMPANY

Chris Carmichael, the world's most famous cycling coach, earned his renown by serving as Lance Armstrong's training and conditioning coach, helping him achieve his seven consecutive wins in the Tour de France. He was part of the inner circle that helped Lance win the Tour after recovering from testicular cancer. When, as Carmichael says, Lance started thinking and talking about "trying to win the Tour," it wasn't something to build a plan on. Not until Lance came to the decision—literally deciding and saying out loud, "I *am* going to win the Tour de France"—did Carmichael get truly engaged. Together with Johan Bruyneel, the director of the US Postal Service and later the Discovery Channel Professional Cycling teams, they developed a program of directed practice and progressive goals that would ultimately lead to Lance wearing the yellow jersey riding on the Champs Elysées in Paris in 7 consecutive years.

It actually started in 1998, when Lance was still recovering from the illness that nearly took his life. Bruyneel introduced to Lance the idea that he was capable of winning the Tour de France. "I remember the moment when he said it to me," Armstrong said. "Johan was the newly named director of the US Postal team, and I was the new team leader. He came to see me in my hotel room at the World Championships and started to talk about his ambitions for me and the team. 'Okay,' he said, 'you just took fourth in Spain, without any special preparation. You just showed up, you didn't even have the ambition to be in the top five, and you ended up fourth. So I think next year we have to work toward [winning] the Tour de France.'"

Lance says that prior to his cancer, he thought he had been doing all that he could with regard to training and competing. But after his illness, he realized that he'd been operating at only about half of his capabilities. He admitted that when he was really honest with himself, he realized that he had never trained as hard or focused as much as he could. He committed to working on becoming a better and more efficient rider. With Bruyneel and Carmichael, he studied proper aerodynamic positioning and effective cadence. "I became an extremely good technical rider," Lance said, "the athlete turned into a trained and practiced cyclist."

Chris Carmichael is much more than the coach who guided Lance Armstrong to peak conditioning and success. A former professional and Olympic cyclist himself and the US Olympic Committee's Coach of the Year in 1999, he is the founder of Carmichael Training Systems, a firm that has coached hundreds of the world's best athletes and top executives in business. He is also the author of three books, most recently *5 Essentials for a Winning Life.*

His insights about natural talent as a factor in the achievement of greatness are applicable to athletic performance, but they are similarly applicable outside of sport. According to Carmichael, there are three categories of high-performing individuals: the talented, the gifted, and the champion.

In the talented performer are someone who achieves some measure of great success simply on the merits of natural ability. Competing at a high school or local level, it is relatively easy to stand out if you have the naturally endowed talents that are germane to the sport or activity.

In the second camp are the gifted. According to Carmichael, "There is just something about these individuals—an X-factor—that separates them from the merely talented. They have it and you know it." Gifted athletes, just like gifted students or professionals, don't have to work as hard as the others to rise through the ranks. They can—and often do—rely on their gifts to reach the top without too much difficulty.

However, being talented or even gifted will get you only so far. In sports, if you are young, talented, and passionate about your sport, you may be recruited to the next level—a college or regional team. Suddenly you find that everyone is a strong athlete. "At this stage," Carmichael says, "you have to work hard and be smart to stand out. You're no longer competing against just a handful of talented people; you're playing against people just like you who were selected from a far greater candidate pool." The same winnowing process takes place at this stage. Through talent, hard work, and mental toughness, you may break through and win a spot at the next level, the national, international, or professional leagues. "At every level," says Carmichael, "there is a weeding-out process, where you go from competing against a handful of stars to competing in a world where everyone is a star.

"The problem for people in the gifted camp is that they can easily grow to rely upon their gifts for their success," says Carmichael. At the highest levels, Carmichael stresses that naturally endowed talents are no longer enough, because everyone at that level is highly competitive, whether on the basis of a talent "endowed" or "earned." The talented—but not gifted—performer who attains this level has had to become accustomed to working hard and doing what it takes to stay in the game, whereas the gifted person hasn't really had to face the same obstacles. As one progresses to ever higher levels, natural ability can actually cease to be an advantage. At the extreme, it can become a hindrance.

According to Carmichael, great champions have both. "They are blessed with the gift of natural talent and they have the awareness and drive to develop and rise above even the best of packs." This is a very special athlete and person. There are many gifted athletes who never amount to champions. Likewise, there are many talented athletes who work their hardest, but just don't have the gifts to rise to the top. "It is the combination that creates the world's best performers," says Carmichael. "These are the truly gifted people who also have the special natural talent but who also have the drive and mentality of less gifted competitors.

"With Lance, this was certainly the case," says Carmichael. "He was very good, but not truly focused until he got cancer. He had the innate gifts; don't forget he was already a world champion. But it was not enough to really distinguish him from the other world-class performers. With Lance and the other greats that I've worked with, there is something greater than their natural gifts. It's what's going on inside their heads. Lance would never have been the kind of champion he is today if he had not been diagnosed with cancer," concludes Carmichael.

Lance agrees. "I never would have won the Tour de France without the disease," he says, "without the struggle and the lessons that I learned during those difficult months. Without the illness," he adds, "I wouldn't have ever known how to focus on my life. I learned to concentrate on the specifics of cycling, the diet, the training, the preparation, the technology, the innovation, the building of a team. The illness really taught me how to build the best team possible, because I was forced to find the best doctors, the best nurses, the best hospitals, the best procedures."

It also helped Lance gain perspective. While he was and continues to be one of the world's best goal setters, establishing uniquely aspirational long-term goals (e.g., win the Tour de France, cure cancer) and setting micro-specific immediate-term objectives (e.g., spend 120 minutes on the bike maintaining a heart rate between 80 and 85 percent of his peak heart rate; consume 3,600 calories today composed of 20 percent protein, 70 percent carbohydrates, and 10 percent fats), he has simultaneously absolved himself of the need to have his success be defined by others.

"The beauty of the illness is that it allowed me to live my life with no expectations. I was truly the underdog, the guy that wasn't given an opportunity to come back. I remember it now as a great challenge. When I was in the hospital and had just finished brain surgery, Chris [Carmichael] came in and asked, 'How you doing?' And I said, 'I'm doing great.' He kind of laughed and said, 'You're really drugged up now. This guy has no idea what's going on.' But I said, 'No, Chris, I really am doing great. You have to understand, I'm at the lowest point in my life. It can only get better.'

"That was an incredibly powerful position to be in."

99 PERCENT

Lance has a simple postcancer philosophy of life: "I now have only good days or great days." This helped him break through the final barrier that holds back many otherwise great competitors: the fear of failure. According to Carmichael, "A lot of athletes give 99 percent, holding just a modicum of themselves back. But that is just not good enough. Oftentimes, when you see an athlete lose, they say something like, 'I know what I will do next time,' or 'I know there were some things I could have done differently.' These are indications that the athlete did not give his or her all during the competition. It is only moments after the game and they are already aware of the fact that they could have performed better. It is the less frequent occasion," notes Carmichael, "that a player says, 'I got beat,' which, in essence, acknowledges that they gave the best performance possible but were just not good enough."

It is a little scary for the aspiring champion to admit that he or she is not as good as a competitor. "People hold back that 1 last percent so they don't have to face not being good enough. If there is always something they could have done better," Carmichael says, "they are still safe."

Those who are able to find that extra 1 percent do so because they are not afraid of failing. They take risks, put themselves on the line, and are prepared to live with the consequences. "What made Michael Jordan able to hit the game-winning three-pointer?" Carmichael asks rhetorically. "Sure he was the guy that had the gifts, the talent, and the drive. But he was also the guy that wanted to take the shot and was not afraid to miss, despite the pressure and public fanfare. You can't make it if you don't shoot it."

Champions want to win, and hate to lose; but they are not *afraid* to lose. "With Lance, after he faced cancer, his outlook on fear was totally different," says Carmichael. "The risk of losing a race was trivialized, if not completely eliminated. I think this really freed him up to give 100 percent of himself."

How applicable is this lesson about sports champions to success in business? Carmichael said that the key element is "not letting fear get in the way. There is so much unknown in business, but you still have to take the shots. Think about the most successful entrepreneurs in this world and how some of the greatest companies were started. The people that started them were talented and had natural gifts and of course they worked hard. But they were also not afraid of taking the major risks."

THE HARD WORK OF SUCCESS

Evading physical discomfort, avoiding conflict, and running away from risk are products of human nature. That is how the majority of us are wired. The lesson from great champions, however, is that only through embracing the pain and hard work of focused training can you then build up the physical and mental strength to make it to the top.

Just about everyone wants to achieve success, but far fewer are prepared to make the necessary sacrifices and put in the requisite effort to succeed to any meaningful degree. Many desperately search for shortcuts, but the outcome is pseudo-success, the appearance of performance that all too often falls apart when the pressure is on and it really counts.

There is no evidence that high-level performance can be achieved without experience built up through practice. A deep body of evidence supports the 10-year rule, the case that even the most talented need those years of hard work before attaining world-class performance. Even Tiger Woods and all of his success starting from an early age is an admirable example of hard work over a long period of time. Because he was introduced to golf at such a young age, and because of a love of the game and parental support, he built up a bank account of 15 years of practice by the time he became the winner of the US Amateur Championships. He accomplished this at 18 years old, the youngest golfer ever to win this prestigious title. Also, he has never stopped working to improve, devoting hours upon hours each day to strength and flexibility conditioning, the technical aspects of his game, and specific shots. He even remade his swing not once, but twice over the past 10 years. Rather than hanging on at the current level, he determined that this was necessary to keep on getting better.

Whether it is playing golf or rugby, litigating, being a chef, or playing the piano, the top performers in the world—the champions—not only work harder than everyone else in their field, but they have invested many more hours of highly focused practice over the years. The chart below, adapted from an influential 1993 study on deliberate practice, shows the relationship between amateurs and experts using pianists as examples.

Deliberate Practice in the Acquisition of Expert Performance

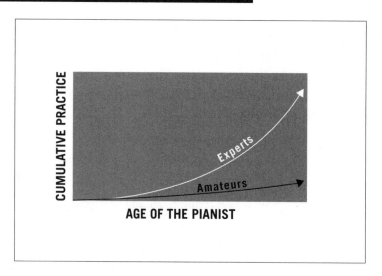

Source: K. Anders Ericsson, department of psychology, Florida State University, *Behavioral and Brain Sciences,* Cambridge University Press, 1998; "The Role of Deliberate Practice in the Acquisition of Expert Performance," K. Anders Ericsson, Ralf Th. Krampe, Clemens Tesch-Römer, *Psychological Review,* 1993.

DELIBERATE PRACTICE

So greatness requires extraordinary hard work on a sustained basis. But some people, even those who also have high levels of natural talent, who do the hard work over a period of years, fail to break through and attain the level of greatness they hoped to achieve. What's missing? The champions in any field are those who devote the most time to what performance experts call deliberate practice. Hard work is fine. But for it to be genuinely effective, the work needs to be directed. Deliberate practice is an activity designed to help you improve a specific skill or performance, to enable you to reach for goals just beyond your level of proficiency, to provide you feedback on results, and to build a program that allows for high levels of repetition.

Bjorn Borg, one of the greatest tennis champions in history, was a proponent of deliberate practice (even if he had no idea of this term at the time he was living it). Borg won Wimbledon a record five consecutive times, including the legendary July 5, 1980, final over archrival John McEnroe. In this "match of endurance and suspense, perhaps unequalled in its athletic splendor, the Swede and American produced the most gripping tiebreaker ever played [18–16]," according to tennis journalist Steve Flink. The seeds of Borg's athletic greatness were planted in his naturally endowed speed and stamina. But it was his consistency and superhuman mental toughness that allowed him to become a champion.

As a 9-year-old, Borg played by himself, up to 7 hours a day, hitting the ball against the garage at his home in Sweden. Rather than just rallying against the wall, however, he played an imaginary Davis Cup match, Sweden versus America. If he was able to hit more than 10 consecutive times, Sweden won the point. Sweden remained undefeated for a very long time. By age 12, Borg was playing 9 hours a day, 7 days a week, working on one stroke until it could be performed with utter confidence in any situation, and only then moving to the next stroke.

Through about 3,000 hours of directed drilling each year, Borg made his strokes automatic, allowing no room for his mind to interfere.

How do you apply deliberate practice in your life? Here's a way to think about it. Let's say you have decided that it's time, once and for all, to become a significantly better golfer. You've found that going to the driving range and hitting two bucketfuls of balls every Saturday hasn't fundamentally improved your game and lowered your handicap. But now, you select a shot to master and design an improvement regimen to get you to that point. Here's what directed practice would look like on the driving range: hitting a pitching wedge to a flag 100 yards away 200 times with the goal of getting the ball to within 10 feet of the pin 80 percent of the time, continually observing results and making appropriate adjustments, and doing that for a couple of hours every weekend until you've reached your goal.

You can do the exact same thing at work. You can think about a few concrete things that are at the core of your role and how to do them significantly better. One divisional president of an investment banking firm did this with his team and in the process achieved not only better results but a markedly improved team culture. He tested various forms of compensation and performance reporting with the goal of having his bankers establish higher-quality, more senior level, and more strategic relationships with their clients. After discussing and prototyping various approaches, he implemented the new system. Rather than measuring and compensating his bankers solely based on their fee production during the year, the new approach was based on setting specific new performance objectives centered around having at least four in-person meetings a quarter with client CEOs or CFOs. Following each client meeting, the bankers were now expected to write detailed call reports, including the length and venue of the meeting, the topics discussed, the documents and ideas presented, new insights garnered about the client's business and professional motivations, and an action plan for the ensuing quarter.

Similar to a college professor, he then carefully reviewed and provided specific feedback on the reports and presented the best ones in weekly staff meetings. It took only 2 months for the culture of the division to change palpably. The greatest honor was now not only bagging the biggest deal, but it was also having your client meeting report circulated and read aloud in front of peers at the staff meeting. Lo and behold, within 2 years, the divisional results had spiked to a new level of financial performance and the firm achieved distinctly stronger competitive positioning in the market.

If you commit to spending a few months focused on how to run much better meetings, for example, you will become a fundamentally more effective manager. Your team will notice. Then you can turn your attention to the next area to improve, whether it's giving presentations to large groups of people, delivering more productive performance reviews, or searching for and testing the best questions to ask in new business situations.

Consistency is fundamental to deliberate practice. It cannot be episodic. "Elite performers in many diverse domains have been found to practice, on the average, roughly the same amount every day, including weekends," according to Dr. Ericsson.

TALENT, HARD WORK, AND SELF-CONFIDENCE

Chris Carmichael has it right when he says that the great champions are those who have both the natural gifts and who also follow deliberate practice over a sustained period of time. Remember Bill Bradley's 25-shots-in-a-row rule and the hours upon hours he spent in the gym every day? This was a key ingredient in his success. But so were his height, peripheral vision, quickness, intelligence, and coolness under pressure. Deliberate practice is simply the best way to make the most of your naturally endowed talents.

Bob Rotella, PhD, the sports psychologist and renowned golf teacher, is mental coach to the New York Yankees, San Francisco 49ers, New Jersey Nets, Texas Rangers, and US Olympic ski and equestrian teams. He directed the country's foremost graduate program in sports psychology at the University of Virginia for 20 years. Today, in addition to consulting with the aforementioned teams, he works with numerous golfers on the PGA Tour, a roster of NASCAR drivers, and many entertainers and business executives. He has also conducted workshops for such leading companies as Merrill Lynch, PepsiCo, and General Electric. Rotella's golfers on the PGA Tour have won at least 25 of the 40 tournaments played for each of the last 15 years. His best-known work is the book *Golf Is Not a Game of Perfect*, one of the three best-selling golf books in history and one of the best-selling sports psychology books ever.

As important as natural talent and hard work through deliberate practice are to meaningful success, Dr. Rotella said that there is one other important and elusive ingredient as well. "It is actually much easier for most people to work hard than it is to believe in themselves," he said. "I think there are so many people who are really talented and hardworking who don't believe in themselves. What strikes me more than anything is that in the American culture, we have sold the importance of the work ethic for years so totally and completely we have lots of people who will work their tail off and yet will choose to never believe in themselves." He offered a historical interpretation for his belief. "When people first came to this country, we had the Puritan work ethic. People thought that if you were having fun doing anything recreational or enjoyable, you were being irresponsible. Later this evolved into the middle-class work ethic. I try to get people to understand that they call it the middle-class work ethic because it's a great way to get into—and stay in—the middle class. But if you want to get the rest of the way, you're going to have to have a greater vision and opinion of yourself."

Dr. Rotella said that he tells his golf students, "Picture yourself as the best golfer in the world." He tells them to suspend their disbelief and just allow themselves to imagine what it would feel like to be the number-one player on the PGA Tour, the number-one money winner, and the recipient of lucrative endorsement contracts. "When you offer them this personal opportunity, the first thing they say is 'Well, Doc, that's silly. If I had Tiger Woods's talent, I'd be a great player and could be the best in the world. After all, I have a great attitude, but I don't have anywhere near the talent.' Then I tell them that they actually have a lousy attitude. There's no way they can have a great attitude if they think that the only way to be the best is to have the talent of Tiger Woods. 'What do you mean?' they ask incredulously. Well, what I mean is that you must believe in your talent, your personality, your potential, and your ability. If there was a base at the pyramid of success, this attitude of believing in yourself would be it."

The easiest way to have confidence is to have always had it—from having been a child prodigy. "If you're successful from an early age and you win consistently by wide margins, that is the easiest way to believe in yourself," Dr. Rotella says. "Most people, however, don't have that in their backgrounds. For all those players who weren't child prodigies, I say, 'Okay, here's *your* life. You weren't a child prodigy. What are you going to do about it? Do you want to use the fact that you haven't won for 10 years as a motivator, or as an excuse? Are you locked into believing that you're not capable of winning, or do you want to figure it out?' I remind people that Jack Nicklaus is still the greatest player in history, and his mom and dad did not bring him up even close to the way Tiger's parents raised him. Jack didn't have his parents telling him every day he was going to be the greatest player in history. It was more like, 'Yeah, that's good you got another trophy, Jack. Now go clean your room, mow the lawn, and then show us your trophy.'

"If you've come to terms with the fact that you weren't given the gift from birth, you still need to develop the confidence that marks the prodigies. If you continue to say, 'Well, I don't have the talent to be the best,' then you have an out, an explanation for why you're not going to be really successful," Dr. Rotella says. "It's the greatest cop-out in the world. It's almost like we've sold people on [the idea that] the greatest thing in the world is to have no talent and outwork everybody. I'd rather have you have a great attitude and work smarter and better than everybody else."

PERCEPTION

So that's what it comes down to: perception. Raw talent and deliberate practice can take you far, but only so far. For even the greatest champions, their perception of themselves, their place in the world, and their chances for success stands on the podium along with talent and dedication. As Carmichael said of Lance Armstrong, it wasn't until he battled cancer and learned what losing was *really* about that he was able to commit himself fully, the risks be damned.

I've experienced this personally at a granular level. At the end of my first week in graduate business school I thought that I wasn't going to be able to cut it. I found my classmates intelligent and articulate to an intimidating degree. The school's grading system was formulated to create anxiety and competition. Half of each and every course grade was determined by your oral contributions made over the course of a semester of daily discussions about a particular business case. For every course, professors were required to implement a forced curve that failed the bottom 10 to 15 percent of each class. And if you failed three classes during the first year, you were not invited back for the second year. During those early days I was frozen, unable to bring myself to make a comment. My 2 hours of preparation for each of the day's three cases went to hell in a handbasket when all of "my" comments were made by others in the first 15 minutes of each class. So I sat silently through the remaining 60 minutes hoping not to get cold-called. Finally, in the second week, I decided I had no choice but to dive into the fray. With my heart pounding, I remember making a wry remark that caused the class to burst out laughing; with that icebreaker, I relaxed and was able to deliver my comment. That was a pattern that I employed in that first semester. The more that I relaxed and came to trust myself, the easier it was to contribute meaningfully (and with the aid of frequent humor, memorably) to the class discussion. I vividly remember coming to realize that playing it safe only heightened anxiety and subpar performance and that putting yourself on the line was more exciting, more effective, and a greater learning experience. The happy footnote is that not only did I not fail out, but I found a way to graduate in the top 10 percent of the class.

So that's the essential idea—the risks be damned. You must perceive that you are indomitable, even if objective reality demurs. You must translate this perception into a core belief in yourself. You *can* win. You are not afraid of failure because you will learn from your fall and it's merely a step on the path to greatness. Sure, you're in the zone. Yes, you've got flow. But really, you're tough. Mentally tough.

This brings us right into the mind of the champion.

CHAPTER 5

The Mind of a Champion

In the 2000 Davis Cup final, Australian tennis star Lleyton Hewitt was battling some sort of virus. He had been having trouble breathing for a couple of months and hadn't been able to do his normal amount of training. His opening match was against Spaniard Alberto Costa—in Barcelona. There were 30,000 Spaniards there, and they were out for Hewitt's blood. The captain of that Australian Davis Cup team, John Newcombe, recalled the story for me:

I knew this match was going to be a war; every point was going to be a war. So just before he went out there, I took him aside and said, 'Lleyton, let me tell you something. About 2 hours into this match, you're going to feel absolutely stuffed; I mean thoroughly exhausted and plain awful. As soon as this happens, you've got to tell me, because I think I can get you out of it. But if you wait too long, it will be too late to do anything.'

After 2 hours and 15 minutes, it went to 3–2 in the third set. Every point was unbelievable. They were going on for so long the crowd was going berserk. The players were working their backs off out there. Lleyton comes over during the changeover and sits down beside me. I was passing him a drink and when he got it in his hand, I could see his whole arm was shaking. He looked at me and said, 'Okay Newk, I'm stuffed.' His whole body was now shaking and his expression was saying, 'All right, you promised. Fix me.'

So, I said, 'Mate, what I want you to do is to take a really deep breath. You've got a lot of negative energy stored up inside you, and you need to get rid of it. I want you to sit back in the chair, close your eyes, and take another really deep breath. Now, when you blow that breath out, what you're blowing out is all this negative, putrid, rotten air and energy that's inside you. Then when you breathe in again, I want you to imagine that up above you is clear, blue sky. What you're breathing down into you is the clearest, strongest air that you've ever had inside your body. Now do it again, because you've still got some of that rotting, stinking stuff inside you. Take another deep breath and blow it out slowly, and breathe in more of that energy that's now gone deep down inside your body. Don't just breathe it into your lungs, bring it right down inside your guts.'

As he did this, he was sitting back, eyes closed, completely relaxed and trusting me. Finally, when he got up out of the chair, I looked deeply into his eyes and said, 'Mate, when you go out on that court now, you are the strongest bastard that's ever lived. You will be able to run forever.' So out he went and play he did. On every change of sides, we did the same thing again. Two hours and 20 minutes later, Lleyton served for the match at 5–4 in the fifth set. He went down love-40, but then he reeled off the next five straight points to win the match!

Newk said that with this approach, Hewitt was running as well at the end of the match as at the beginning. He knew this was possible for Hewitt because it was an experience that he had been through in the past himself. "Anyone can reach inside their belly to draw up those reserves that are in there," Newcombe said, "but you've got to know how to tap into them." A year later, Hewitt played in the Masters final in Shanghai against Spain's Juan Carlos Ferrero. He was down a break in the fifth and final set and was absolutely exhausted. Newk wasn't there to help him, but Hewitt was able to do the same thing by doing it to himself. And he came back to win the match.

Mental toughness is the powerful ingredient that separates the journeyman from the champion. Along with natural talent and a dedicated and directed work ethic, it is the final major component in the making of a champion.

I can say confidently that even among the world's most accomplished and renowned athletes, there is a perceptible difference between the good and the truly great. The difference is mental toughness, the obsession to win, the killer instinct. There *is* something different. Lance Armstrong sits atop of this pinnacle along with only a few others, including Michael Jordan, Tiger Woods, and perhaps Roger Clemens. Mark Gorski was a cycling gold medalist in the 1984 Olympics and CEO of Tailwind Sports, the management and marketing company that ran the US Postal Service team that employed Lance. When I interviewed Gorski, he said, "Lance *is* different. Other racers, even great ones, lumber to the top of the treacherous debilitating climbs and are content just to win, sometimes even just to finish. But not Lance. When he gets up to the top, he doesn't want to just win. He wants to crush you. To rip your guts out."

When I asked Lance about the killer instinct and where the fire comes from, he thought for a moment and then said, "It has always burned brightly in me. I think it comes from growing up in difficult circumstances." He added, "This was not only the case for me, but for the other guys, Michael Jordan, Tiger Woods, and Roger Clemens as well. They and many of the other greatest athletes grew up poor and wanted to use sports to break out. That creates a profound desire within to succeed; it certainly fired me up."

As depicted in the "Composition of a Champion" graphic below, the champion is equal parts natural talent, work ethic, and mental toughness. Increasing your mental toughness will enable you to win more and derive greater enjoyment from competing. It is all about learning to play in a more instinctive way and not being intimidated by the ups and downs of a competition. While Lance attributes the ferocious ability to win to difficult circumstances early in life, the fact is that anyone can learn to become much tougher mentally and a more frequent winner. Whether you are an aspiring player or a professional in sports or a manager or CEO in business, this chapter will show you how to think correctly and *apply* this thinking through directed practice. That, along with your naturally endowed talents and the lessons learned in Chapter 4, will in turn allow you to achieve your best as a competitor, become the most accomplished performer in sport, or be the most valuable contributor in business.

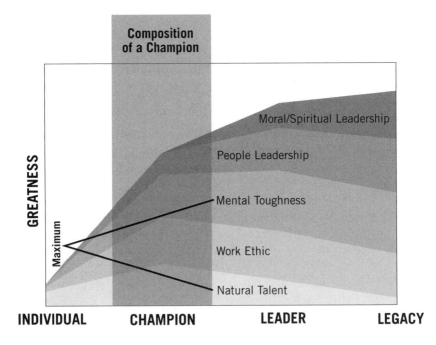

THE TRUTH ABOUT WINNING

While you can't do much about your innate talent, how you think and how you apply your natural talent have nothing to do with genetics. Becoming a better thinker and more effective competitor is much more in your control than you may realize.

During my research, I happened across a little book called *The Truth about Winning*. A mere 79 pages long, it could be the most influential book I've read since Stephen Covey's *The Seven Habits of Highly Effective People*. Written by Tom Veneziano, a creative and literary tennis pro in Texas, it is intended to help players win on the tennis court. It turns out that the insights and methods it describescan be applied not only to tennis, but to competing in any other sport, coaching youth sports, even to business. For me now, barely a week goes by when I don't apply Veneziano's lessons.

Winning, as anyone who has been truly successful will tell you, depends on a robust history of failure. I know it sounds counterintuitive, but to learn how to win, you must learn how to lose correctly. Don't lose on purpose, but practice having the correct mental attitude toward mistakes and losses. Veneziano says, "Until you accomplish this, forget everything else." No technical training or game strategy will help you improve at a fundamental level. You must give yourself the freedom to go for your shots, and if you miss, accept it. The great champions learn to do this, and that is how they can give their utmost to a competition; the principal safety net is their own mental resilience.

This attitude frees you to keep fighting, to keep challenging yourself, and to keep taking risks. You don't want your mistakes to be so important in your mind that they stop you from performing. Practicing the right attitude during and after mistakes and losses is a top priority. If you are thinking correctly, you won't be worrying about the results, and they will eventually take care of themselves. Winning is actually the easy part. The hard part is thinking correctly and doing so continuously.

NEGATIVES *ARE* NEGATIVE
WHEN EMOTIONS DICTATE

It takes longer to reach your goals if you don't assess mistakes—or negatives—productively. Properly assessed, negatives give you valuable feedback, allowing you to make corrections so that the mistake does not repeat itself. It is perfectly fine to recognize and analyze negatives when they occur. But it is essential to stop thinking that acknowledging negatives, mistakes, or failures is a sign of weakness. The ability to think about mistakes and stay confident is a sign of strength, not weakness.

Mentally tough people don't let negatives affect their attitudes. They view negatives, mistakes, and losses for what they are—sources of important information necessary to reach their goals. The almost shockingly obvious reality is that mistakes, losses, and failures are always there, even for the best performer in the world. Roger Federer occasionally hits the easy overhead into the net, just as Tiger misses the 3-foot putt and Michael Jordan missed back-to-back free throws. If these happen to the world's best, it only makes sense that it happens to you, too. Remind yourself that you are not unique in blowing the easy opportunity.

There is a reason that people get so upset by making errors—beyond immediately thinking that it will cause them to lose. How often do you hear someone say to himself or herself after an unforced error, "I blew it. I stink." Is that someone ever you? How about tightening up when you "should" win a match, a competition, or an account and unraveling when things don't go your way? The reason for these thoughts is that if you are like most others, you are being guided by your emotions rather than your mind. Moreover, you exaggerate the emotional response by linking mistakes to who you are as a person. Either consciously or subconsciously, your emotional reactions in a performance arena lead you to think that if you perform poorly, you are a bad person.

Let me let you in on something: Just because things work out poorly does not mean you have done something wrong. More importantly, there is absolutely no connection between your ability or results in a competition and your quality or character as a person.

This is just as true when you win. If things work out well, it does not necessarily mean that you have done something right. Just as most people pair losing with doing something incorrectly, they similarly link winning with doing something correctly. This, too, is often erroneous. When you win on a lucky break or low-percentage shot, your emotions will cause you to conclude, "I won. That was a good play. I am good."

Emotional play leads you to think short-term, not long-term, seeking out immediate gratification at the expense of strategy. Your emotions deceive you into believing that the way to win is to hit a winner, even if you have no business hitting that shot. Winning emotionally will catch up with you eventually, and you won't know what to do about it. Emotions don't provide long-term consistency, which is necessary for winning when it counts.

When you stop to think about it, however, it is ridiculous to think that the ability or results you enjoy in any environment determine your quality or character as a person. There is no connection between the two. This simple but profound insight—decoupling your results and your self-worth—can, in and of itself, free you up to be a more natural and mentally tough competitor in all aspects of life.

REFOCUSING IN THE WAKE OF DISTRACTIONS

Recovering from emotional outbursts after mistakes is genuinely difficult. But having the ability to regain composure and do so quickly is one of the most important attributes of the mind of the champion. Performance expert and sports psychologist Terry Orlick, PhD, said, "If I were asked to choose one mental skill that distinguishes top performers who remain at the top of their game, I would name their ability to adapt and refocus in the face of distraction."

Distractions come not only from making mistakes. They can also come from thinking that you are going to win or taking your mind off of what you are doing and focusing on your competitors. If you start to compare how you are performing relative to your own expectations or those of family, coaches, colleagues, or competitors, you will quickly become distracted. Any number of things can cause you to lose the focus that allows you to apply your skills effectively. The key is how you recover.

First a fundamental point. You don't *lose* your abilities or skills because of something that distracts you. You *allow* yourself to become distracted and *thereby* lose the ability to execute properly. So how do you get back on track? Through these four actions:

▶ Commit yourself to being guided by your mind rather than your emotions. This is equally true in going up against a competitor for a new piece of business and in challenging an opponent on the field or court.

▶ Rehearse getting into a positive state of mind before practice sessions and performances and staying focused on the job at hand over the course of the event or meeting.

▶ Expect others to behave differently in high-stakes competitions or situations. Even those who are normally cool and collected may become undone by their own self-imposed pressure. In other words, the same pressure that you feel to perform is also being experienced by your opponent or competitor. Chances are that someone is going to crack under the pressure; it might just as well be them.

▶ Find a mantra that helps you recover the right state of mind. For example, when you are sliding into negativity on the tennis court, Veneziano suggests repeating the following:

THE NEXT SHOT IS MORE IMPORTANT THAN THE LAST MISTAKE.
TO BE GOOD, I HAVE TO MAKE MISTAKES.

In a work setting, these steps work similarly well. Recognize that the more you use your mind rather than your emotions to solve whatever problem comes up, the better off you will be. If you watched the film *Apollo 13*, you can picture the kind of dispassionate problem solving displayed by the astronauts and mission control under unimaginable pressure. They had rehearsed and drilled, which allowed their minds rather than their emotions to guide their actions and decisions in the heat of the moment.

Don't be surprised when a setback affects you or your team and plan for it ahead of time. Find a mantra that helps you through the difficult situations that inevitably come up. I've done this many times, and it has helped me get back on track at crucial moments. For example, if a deal falls through at the final stages of a recruitment process and we have to "restart" the search, I say the following words to myself:

THE MORE DIFFICULT THE ASSIGNMENT IS TODAY,
THE MORE MEMORABLE IT WILL BE LATER.

This has helped me, various teams, and clients recover from deep disappointment when having to restart an important project and gather the intensity and motivation to begin afresh. I've had to completely restart an important search about 20 times over the years, such as when an accepted offer was countered and a candidate reneged on an agreement, or a candidate committed to join the new organization only to pull out when the individual's spouse or family broke down at the news of relocating, or the client decided that it wanted to see "just one more candidate" and the finalist decided that she didn't want to go forward if the hiring company wasn't sufficiently confident to commit *right now*.

Following the aforementioned steps will enable you to shift from thinking with your emotions to thinking with your mind, in business and in sports. It takes time, patience, and repetition to put these concepts into practice because the conflict between emotions and the mind is real and continuous. Getting it right, however, is worth the effort because you will be one of the few who understand how to deal with negatives correctly, which will accrue to your advantage in sports and business.

POSITIVE IMAGERY

"MY THEORY HAS ALWAYS BEEN THAT IF YOU REALLY WANT SOMETHING, IF YOU CAN SEE IT, IF YOU CAN VISUALIZE IT AND YOU ARE WILLING TO PAY THE PRICE OF VERY HARD WORK, THEN YOU CAN ACHIEVE IT."
—HERB MCKENLEY
Jamaica track, Olympic silver medalist,
1948 London, gold and double silver medalist, 1952 Helsinki

Applying positive imagery allows you not only to refocus when necessary, but also to prepare yourself to remain focused right from the start. It allows you to react in constructive ways, to feel the flawless execution of your desired performance, to create positive feelings about yourself, take corrective actions, and enhance your self-confidence. Pretty powerful stuff.

Through positive imagery, you can experience feelings, sensations, skills, and actions that will be important when it comes to actual performance. High-quality images of your best fairway iron, free throw, downhill run, or client presentation allow you to experience yourself doing it right and help you feel ready to perform to your highest skill level. These multisensory images take you where you want to go and often where you have not yet been.

Dr. Bob Rotella tells the story of two young golfers sharing a room on the PGA tour. "After the practice round on one course with lightning-fast greens, a young Gary Player told Davis Love II, 'I love these greens! You just touch the ball and it goes right to the hole. They are my favorite kind of greens.' Love thought how fortunate Player was to find those challenging greens to his natural liking. Back in their room after the practice round of the following week's tournament, on a course with slow bent-grass greens, Player exclaimed, 'I love these greens! You can take a full stroke and power the ball right into the hole.' When Love quizzically asked how he could be so inconsistent, Player looked at him as if he had no idea what he was talking about."

The lesson: Consistent logic is much less important than positive imagery when it comes to setting yourself up to pursue ambitious goals.

Ted Williams, probably the best hitter in the history of Major League Baseball and the last player to hit over .400 in a season (1941), also used positive imagery to pursue his goals. Obsessive about studying opposing pitchers, searching for telltale clues about what they intended to throw and their pitching patterns, he would imagine what a pitcher was going to throw him and exactly how he would react. This wasn't something he was taught in the majors. He did it all his life from the time he played in the backyard when he was a kid.

Many of the world's best performers, including athletes, musicians, astronauts, surgeons, military leaders, and business leaders, have highly developed imagery skills that they use on a daily basis. They use positive imagery to prepare for high-quality performances, recall and refine technical skills, make corrections, relax, experience themselves as successful and in control, regain control when struggling, set a positive frame of mind, and create a high-quality focus.

✦

Joan Benoit-Samuelson—
Marathon Champion, Role Model, and the State of Maine's Proudest Citizen

The circumference of the Earth at the equator is 24,901.6 miles. Over the 30 years of her running career, Joan Benoit-Samuelson estimates that she has run about 120,000 miles. That's circumnavigating the globe nearly five times. One of the most admired and respected distance runners in history, Benoit won the first-ever women's Olympic Marathon on August 5, 1984, in Los Angeles.

Born in Cape Elizabeth, Maine (home of the world's most photographed lighthouse), Benoit grew up an athletic and active girl. "My dad was in the [Army's] 10th Mountain Division," Benoit says, "so he brought us up on skis as soon as we were able to walk." She also ran and played field hockey, basketball, and tennis. It was a quite competitive family. "I have three brothers, so it was survival of the fittest from the get-go." To help recover from a broken leg suffered while ski racing, Benoit started long-distance running in high school and thrived at the sport.

Unfortunately, when she attended Bowdoin College, following in the footsteps of her father and one of her older brothers, the elite Division III liberal arts college did not have a cross-country team. So she played field hockey and ran with the Liberty Athletic Club out of Cambridge, Massachusetts, traveling most weekends with the team. The training worked wonders. As a senior in 1979, she entered her first marathon, the classic Boston Marathon. A virtual unknown, she won, setting an American women's record with a time of 2:35:15. In perhaps the greatest public relations event in the college's history, millions of people saw Benoit cross the finish line wearing a Bowdoin singlet. When she came back to campus the following day and walked into the dining hall, everyone stood up and gave her a standing ovation. "I just wasn't expecting that. To be honest, I was just testing myself with the marathon distance. I didn't understand how big an event Boston was."

Her punishing training regime led to injuries, but her fierce determination and love of the sport kept her at it. She underwent surgery on her Achilles tendons, and then went on again to win the Boston Marathon in 1983. In that race, she broke the world record of Norwegian marathon legend Grete Waitz by more than 2 minutes. Thirteen months later, in May 1984, Benoit won the US Olympic Trials marathon, only 17 days after arthroscopic knee surgery. This set the stage for her dramatic Olympic victory, clocking 2:24:52 in hot and smoggy conditions, finishing more than a minute ahead of the prerace favorites and archrivals Waitz, Rosa Mota, and Ingrid Kristiansen. In recognition of Benoit's accomplishments and her ability to overcome injuries, she received the 1985 James E. Sullivan Award, given to the top amateur athlete in the United States.

Among women runners, Benoit's name is at the top of the list for mental toughness, hard work, and perseverance. "When you talk about mental toughness," Benoit says, "you can put 10 runners on the line, and whoever wants it the most will win. I firmly believe that in the summer of 1984, leading up to the Olympics, nobody was training any harder than I was. This gave me enough confidence to go out and run without hesitation or anxiety."

Beyond marathon championships, an Olympic gold medal, and world records, Benoit has achieved one of the other greatest honors in sports: having her picture grace the front of a Wheaties box (it was in celebration of the Boston Marathon's 100th anniversary). Despite all of her success, Joan Benoit-Samuelson is one of the most down-to-earth champions I have ever met. She is also one of the most driven; her competitive fire still burns brightly. "I have one more goal left in running, and that is to run a sub-2:50 marathon in the Olympic trials at age 50." She's on track, having qualified for the 2008 Olympic trials, which are aptly going to be held in Boston. "I could come full circle and end my career where I started," she says with a smile.

THE KEY TO DEVELOPING MENTAL TOUGHNESS

Top performers play so well under pressure as a result of training themselves for years to think objectively, evaluate realistically, and come to correct conclusions. Most people think that mental toughness is the same thing as never giving up, exercising fierce determination, or maintaining perseverance. While these traits accurately *describe* a mentally tough person, they are not the way *to become* mentally tough. The attributes of mental toughness arise from a deep pool of accumulated wisdom about the objective reality of a competitive situation. They are the qualities of the dispassionate, emotionless person who has built a storehouse of information about competition.

Typically, it takes players years and years of competition coupled with trial and (a lot of) error to develop mental toughness. Happily, you don't have to go through such a long and tortuous process. You can start right now and cut years off of the learning curve by adjusting your thinking in two simple ways:

▶ You do not win by trying to win.

▶ Tennis (or golf, or any sport, or business) repeats itself, so lighten up.

In sports, most people think that the way to win is by doing something spectacular or exciting. They think that hitting home runs in baseball, making birdies in golf, and hitting winners in tennis are the ways to win. If this is your mindset during a match, however, you will try to do too much with the ball every time it comes to you: You *are* going to win the point now. You *have to* go for the green to get on in regulation.

That is the way most of us have been taught to try to win. If this sounds familiar, then you won't be surprised to learn that based on this mindset, this is how you make decisions in the heat of the moment—any moment. Your inevitable mistakes will join your heated emotions, and disappointment will result.

Instead of being mentally tough, you are mentally rigid. You become overanxious—even when you just want to keep the ball in play. If the tennis ball comes back two or three times and you haven't put it away, you think that you've done something wrong. So you try to hit a winner on the next shot—even if it's the wrong time.

The mentally tough player is guided by a disciplined mind. It takes the same kind of deliberate practice to resist the temptation to go for winners at the wrong times as it does to develop your skillset in the first place. You don't have to do something exciting to win. Making birdies, hitting home runs, or doing something spectacular is a *result,* not a cause. You don't win tennis matches by hitting winners, nor do you win golf tournaments by making birdies or baseball games by hitting home runs. Want evidence? A typical winner on the PGA Tour will make about 15 to 20 birdies over a 4-day tournament, only 5 to 7 percent of the holes played. Winning comes much more from the 270 or so pars over the course of the tournament. In tennis, even at the most advanced levels, it is estimated that only about 20 percent of all points are won with outright winners. That's all.

You will take a major step forward in your effort to be mentally tough simply by realizing that winners don't win matches. If you hit a shot that you will make only one out of five times, recognize that for what it is. If you happen to pull it off, great, but be aware that it was an exception. You can't build a long-term game plan around exceptions. Of course, if you are not up to the challenge from a purely physical or natural talent point of view, it can be difficult to see being there mentally. Regardless, mental toughness will improve your performance no matter what your skill level.

So stop trying to win by trying to win. This is the difference between trying to make it happen and letting it happen. The greatest competitors let it happen. If they see opportunities, they seize them. Letting it happen means not trying to hit winners. It means playing steadily, moving the ball around and looking for openings. It means keeping the ball on the fairway, making solid contact with the ball, two-putting. It means being consistent.

Translated to a business context, consistency, dependability, and meeting expectations are what counts in establishing a solid foundation for long-term performance. Successful professionals are those whom others count on to deliver time and time again. They understand their objectives and responsibilities and complete them in a top-quality way. With this foundation laid, moreover, you put yourself in a position to break through to an even higher level of success by differentiating yourself from the other strong performers.

While most people in the workplace are focused on accomplishing the tasks assigned to them and meeting the expectations set by their bosses, the more successful professionals consistently overdeliver. If their quota for a month is 100, they strive to deliver 120. If their project timeline calls for 3 months to completion, they commit to finishing in 10 weeks. These kinds of results are what the vast majority of working people think of when they envision what they have to do to succeed.

There is a variation on this theme, however, that is the equivalent of making a birdie after a string of pars or hitting the winner after 10 smart shots in a rally. That is, rather than simply overdelivering on their stated objectives, the truly extraordinary professionals accomplish what is expected of them in a top-quality way and then find other ways to add value that no one necessarily thought to ask of them. In other words, they do what is expected of them, but rather than just doing more of the same, they do something unexpected that is positive for the organization and, in the process, differentiates themselves from everyone else. Examples of this behavior abound among the most successful professionals. This ranges from the new employee who organizes the summer picnic with an upbeat attitude, to the marketing director who gives a compelling speech at an industry conference, to the chief operating officer who joins a major corporate board and brings new perspectives back into the company. These kinds of activities are icing on the cake of the consistent, dependable, high-quality work at the core of your responsibilities.

GIVE YOUR *OPPONENT* THE OPPORTUNITY TO LOSE

Create and maintain an environment that gives your *opponent* the greatest potential to crack under pressure. If everything you do and think is subordinate to this goal, you *will* become a mentally tough person and you *will* win much more frequently. To accomplish this, you need to handle negatives correctly and recover your focus quickly when you become distracted. You need to master the tendency to try to win and aim for consistency instead. If you become discouraged by mistakes or preoccupied during a competition, the only environment you will create is one in which you—not your opponent—will be prone to cracking. To make this instinctive, you need to focus on this and work to create and maintain the correct environment day after day, month after month.

Someone who did this to an intimidating extreme was Bjorn Borg. His unrivaled consistency and ability to out-concentrate any player in the world was what separated him from the pack of the other great players of his day. He controlled virtually everything that was in his power to control and cultivated in himself the ability to accept those things that he could not control and let them go. Not only was he in command of his on-court concentration, he also meticulously planned his pretournament rituals. For example, he stayed in the same room at the same London hotel during every Wimbledon fortnight and wore the same thing to sleep in each night. Each day before his match, he lined up his 50 Donnay racquets on the floor of his room in order of the tension of the strings as determined by their musical pitch. He then selected just the right tool for the day's job. Out on the court, Borg never questioned a line call—ever. And when a point, game, or set was over, it was over, as far in the past as were his imaginary Davis Cup matches against the garage wall.

Giving your opponent the greatest potential to crack under pressure will enable you to maximize your naturally endowed talents and skills. An opponent, even one who is "better," will more often than not lose to you. He will become more prone to making mistakes, getting overanxious, and cracking under pressure. Champions realize that the seemingly inconspicuous bad decisions a player makes eventually add up and become the difference between winning and losing.

MICHELLE WIE'S CHALLENGE

Just as you cannot be a successful professional without delivering results, you can't be a champion without winning. At its most basic definition, "a champion is one who wins first place in a competition." With that as a backdrop, let's consider how teenage golf phenom Michelle Wie is doing on the path to greatness and the first stop, becoming a champion.

It seems almost preordained that Michelle Wie is positioned to become the "next" Tiger. The comparison is so natural: young, physically gifted, attractive role models who transcend racial, ethnic, and gender lines; media sensations who were both reared by ambitious parents to become the greatest golfers ever. While the similarity is robust, a careful examination of their respective youths and track records to date suggests that the comparison is at best premature.

Wie started playing golf at 4 years old under the tutelage of her father, B.J. Wie. By the time she was 11, with her supernatural ball-striking capabilities, awe-inspiring distance, and understanding of the game, she was winning many of the local amateur tournaments in which she played, even those against adult men. After watching Tiger Woods and with the enthusiastic support of her parents, Wie decided she wanted to become a pro golfer. Her father left his job to work full-time as her coach and business manager. On March 1, 2002, Wie played in her first LPGA tour event, the Takefuji Classic in Hawaii. Although she failed to make the cut, she was still an immediate sensation with her amazing youth, her radiant smile atop her 6-foot height, and her 280-yard drives.

In June 2003, Wie became the youngest winner ever in the Women's Amateur Public Links, an important tournament that brought together the best players from public golf courses around the country. When she teed off at the Sony Open on January 15, 2004, she became the youngest person, and just the fourth female, to play in a PGA tour event. Despite averaging 271 yards on her drives and finishing with a score better than 47 other competitors, Wie missed the 36-hole cut by just one stroke. She also came close to making her first cut at a PGA Tour event at the 2005 John Deere Classic, but a late collapse in the second round led to her missing the cut by two strokes. To date, Wie has played in nearly 30 professional events, and although she has yet to win any, she has had top-five finishes at each of the four LPGA majors. When I asked Dr. Bob Rotella to assess Michelle Wie's performance at this early stage of her career, he said, "If the goal is to make a lot of money, it looks pretty good. But I wouldn't suggest the Wie approach if the goal is to achieve excellence." Indeed. With major endorsement contracts including Nike, Omega, and Sony, Forbes estimates her annual earnings at $17 million. "Watching her play," Dr. Rotella continues, "I'm not sure that Michelle Wie yet believes in herself. Great golfers have a great short game and a great mind. So she's going to have to learn to believe in herself more, and she's going to have to get better with her putter, because every golf tournament finishes with a putt."

Of course it's very difficult to learn how to win while under the microscope. The more customary experience of those who become champions is to learn how to win with no one watching and then become famous, continue to win, and learn how to deal with all of the expectations and pressures.

Part of the reason why Wie has not yet learned to win, according to Dr. Rotella, is that she skipped the big junior age group events and wasn't able to build the deep foundation of success that comes with winning those tournaments against the best players. You develop real mental strength from competing against your own age group. There are many strong emotions that come along with playing against your peers, such as dealing with jealousy and envy. Wie has been shielded from those pressures. "As long as she plays against adult women or guys," Dr. Rotella says, "anything she does is looked at as positive. There's a lot less pressure when you can play to make the cut when everyone else is trying to win the tournament."

Tiger Woods was also a highly visible child prodigy. He began to play golf at the age of 2. In 1978, at age 3, his golf skills were put on display in a television appearance on *The Mike Douglas Show*. At age 5, he was featured in *Golf Digest* magazine. But while he was the subject of such media attention, he also started winning at a young age and hasn't stopped winning ever since. In 1984, when he was only 8 years old, he won the 9- to 10-year-old boys' event at the Junior World Golf Championships. Woods went on to win the junior world championships six times, including four consecutive wins from 1988 to 1991. Woods then won the US Junior Amateur title in 1991, 1992, and 1993. To this day, he remains the event's youngest-ever as well as the only multiple winner. He then won three consecutive US Amateur titles over the next 3 years, the only person ever to achieve this feat, and was also the youngest player ever to win that event. In 1994, he enrolled at Stanford University, where he stayed for 2 years, winning one NCAA individual golf championship.

His professional track record is equally historic. As of March 2007, Woods has won 75 professional tournaments, including 55 PGA Tour events. At 30 years and 7 months old, he was the youngest to reach the 50-win mark. Finally, with 12 major victories, he trails only Jack Nicklaus (with 18) in this, the ultimate metric of golf greatness.

"So when people try to compare Michelle to Tiger," says Dr. Rotella, "my response is that Tiger won everything and at every age group. She certainly hits the ball far, and she's certainly a nice player for her age; you can't take that away. She seems to be a delightful young lady, and it seems like she comes from a very nice family. But when you talk about success in terms of winning, she hasn't yet had it."

In some ways, suggesting that Michelle Wie will become the next Tiger reminds me of another grandiose comparison from the mid-1970s. When a telegenic Scottish pop band named the Bay City Rollers broke onto the American music scene with a couple of top-10 songs on the UK charts, they were heralded as being "the next Beatles." But while they achieved commercial success and even charted a number-one song in 1976, their impact on music and culture was anything but enduring.

That, to me, encapsulates Michelle Wie's challenge: to become a champion in her own right. Not to become the next Tiger or anyone else. But to become the player and the person she is so clearly capable of becoming.

CHAPTER 6

Dynamic Moment II

The Perilous Perch

Over his 13 seasons with the Dallas Cowboys, from 1990 to 2003, and two seasons with the Arizona Cardinals, from 2003 to 2005, Emmitt Smith ran for 18,355 yards, an NFL record. He also set the record with 166 rushing touchdowns; his 175 total touchdowns ranks him second in history behind Jerry Rice, the 49ers receiver who made it into the end zone a total of 207 times. Smith helped lead the Cowboys to three Super Bowl championships and was the first player in NFL history to rush for more than 1,000 yards in 11 consecutive seasons. And right now, in his sun-drenched office in a glass office tower in Dallas, I was being blinded by his Super Bowl ring—as, I suspect, was he.

How do you ever distract yourself from that incredible sparkle to turn your attention to what is next? That is the problem Smith faced, and he is not alone. Countless stellar individual performers find it difficult to turn from their glittering achievements to the unfamiliar challenges and hard work to come.

Call it a midlife crisis. A crossroads. Or a dynamic moment. At some point, everyone, even the world's greatest champion, has to change in order to progress. They can either grow, moving onward and upward along The Dynamic Path, or recede, resigned to having their best days fade away into an increasingly idealized past.

By the time Emmitt Smith and I met, I had done enough research on sports leaders to recognize that the patterns between sports stars and business leaders were strikingly similar. Only 36, Smith wanted to continue to grow and develop, but he knew he would have to change. He needed to take his experiences and assets developed from a prodigious career to date and find ways to apply them to one or more new situations that highly value those experiences.

So we turned the conversation on its head. Instead of solely interviewing Smith for this book, we started talking about which sports champions successfully made the transition from one stage to another and who had failed and why. We also talked about how some business leaders continued to grow and develop while others faded into oblivion.

What Smith and I discussed was how careers really work. Careers generally have three phases—the "promise" phase, the "momentum" phase, and the "harvest" phase. Individuals have two related but distinct sources of value that combine to determine their degree of success at each stage. At the beginning of your career, your value is almost entirely dependent on your potential—how much you will be able to contribute to the organization in the future. When you are hired fresh out of college, the basis of your value is your potential—your natural talents, intellect, interpersonal skills, ambition, and the like. Over the course of the early part of your career, as you start to gain more professional experience, your success is determined less and less by your potential and more and more by the actual experience that you develop.

As you move forward in business, your success becomes much more dependent on your track record. This is the flywheel of your career that I call the momentum phase. If you are a marketing executive, this is when you build brands, manage new product introductions and advertising campaigns, create and optimize customer segmentations, and open up new channels for customer acquisition. If you are a finance executive, this is when you manage the preparation of financial statements, take a company public, establish banking relationships, manage risk, and lead acquisitions. The more experience you have in your area of expertise, the more you will be valued by your current organization and, incidentally, by other organizations looking to recruit top executives.

At some point in the momentum phase—in business this is usually at about the age of 45 to 55—there comes a time when careers begin to diverge. Some individuals manage to keep developing personally and professionally, moving into new positions or redefining their existing roles. Many others, however, start to recede. They get passed over for new opportunities or find themselves in a rut. Even though they might be doing what they have always done and doing it well, their careers seem to be headed sideways or south toward retirement. This is another dynamic moment. Those who are able to move into the harvest—or final—phase of their careers amid ever-increasing success do so by discovering a way to take their experiences and apply them to new situations.

Understanding how career paths evolve will help you progress along The Dynamic Path. As illustrated in the career trajectory chart on page 104, for each stage—champion, leader, and legacy—there is an important interaction between your potential and your experience. Your individual natural talents are the equivalent of potential value. Through hard work, dedication, and mental toughness, you apply your talents to build up a track record. This is the equivalent of your experiential value. Winning often enough will earn you the designation of champion. Or succeeding consistently in important-enough ways will turn you into the most highly valued of professionals. The same interaction between potential and experience holds true for the leader and the legacy builder. At each stage, there is an equivalent type of potential—the ability to work through and inspire others, for example—that has to be exercised and applied, the results of which are the impact, or experiential value, that you've achieved.

Career Trajectory

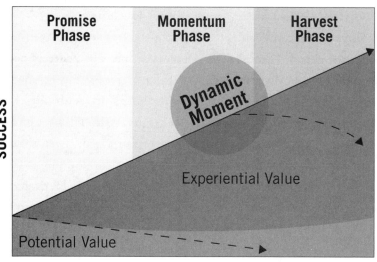

✦

Senator George Mitchell—
The Building Blocks of Career Success

When Senator George Mitchell graduated from Maine's Bowdoin College in 1954 or Georgetown's law school in 1960, he had no idea that one day he would become the lead investigator into steroid abuse for Major League Baseball. Nor could he have imagined becoming chairman of The Walt Disney Company, US Senate majority leader, or chief negotiator to bring peace between Northern Ireland and Ireland. Had he set his sights on these lofty leadership positions, he almost surely would have come up short.

Despite exhortations of some career experts to set specific long-term career goals with interim milestones to measure your success, this is not how extraordinary careers usually unfold. Whether in sports or business, great careers are built block by block, experience by experience; exceptional performance at one stage opens up opportunities for the next. Often, as in the case of Senator Mitchell, the subsequent possibility couldn't have even been imagined before it presented itself.

Only in retrospect can extraordinary careers be understood logically, as in the case of Senator Mitchell. With his legal training, he got the opportunity to serve as a trial attorney at the Antitrust Division of the US Department of Justice. After 2 years as part of the community of young lawyers in Washington, he became executive assistant to Maine senator Edmund S. Muskie from 1962 to 1965, giving him his first exposure to the workings of America's most exclusive club, the US Senate. He then returned to Portland, Maine, and practiced law for 12 years until he was appointed to the United States Senate in 1980 to complete the unexpired term of Senator Muskie, who traded in his position in the Senate to become secretary of state. Senator Mitchell was elected to a full term in the Senate in 1982 and went on to an illustrious career spanning 14 years.

In 1988, he was reelected with 81 percent of the vote, the largest margin in Maine history. Given the bipartisan respect he earned and maintained during his tenure, he was elected to become Senate majority leader in 1989, a position he held until he left the Senate in 1995. For 6 consecutive years he was voted "the most respected member" of the Senate by a bipartisan group of senior congressional aides. He further distinguished himself as chairman of the peace negotiations in Northern Ireland. Under his leadership, the governments of Ireland and the United Kingdom and the political parties of Northern Ireland agreed on a historic accord, ending decades of conflict. In May 1998, the voters of Ireland, north and south, overwhelmingly endorsed the agreement in a referendum. With Senator Mitchell's diplomacy track record having been established, President Bill Clinton, Israeli Prime Minister Ehud Barak, and Palestine Liberation Organization chairman Yasser Arafat subsequently requested that he serve as chairman of an international fact-finding committee that examined the Israeli-Palestinian crisis.

Senator Mitchell's credibility later made him the ideal choice to become chairman of the board of The Walt Disney Company at the moment when the chairman and CEO roles needed to be separated to address shareholder concerns. After guiding the highly successful CEO succession process at Disney, he was able to step off the board and focus on his responsibilities with Major League Baseball and as a partner in the Washington law firm of DLA Piper Rudnick Gray Cary.

One important lesson from Senator Mitchell's extraordinary career is to adopt a new way to evaluate dynamic moments and career turning points. Ask the question, "Will this new role (or project or company) increase the number of options likely to become available to me in the future?" If the answer to this is "yes," that is much of what you need to know to encourage you to accept the opportunity. Answering "no" does not automatically mean that you should say no; however, it does suggest that you need to be certain that a narrowed set of future alternatives is something you are comfortable with.

Emmitt Smith's challenge is simpler yet simultaneously more complex than Senator Mitchell's. He has fame and hero status from his NFL career as well as from an improbably yet highly successful stint on the hit television show *Dancing with the Stars*. However, Smith's transformation will be even less linear: There is no business in need of exactly the same skills he displayed on the gridiron. As with many—if not most—successful individual performers, Smith must learn how to apply the attributes and experience that earned him champion status to a group of new challenges. However, that is only part of what constitutes the second dynamic moment. As challenging as it was to become a champion, it is arguably more difficult to leave the comfort and attention of this stage and refract the energy that people directed toward you onto others. At this point you must not only evolve your own skills, you must also let go of individual achievement. From now on, what you achieve, you achieve through others.

As we are being battered by the wave of disappointing revelations from our sports champions, from college football players being convicted of assault and battery and betting on games, to professional cyclists and track stars being stripped of their championships and world records for doping, to a formal investigation by Major League Baseball into the use of performance-enhancing drugs, it is fair to ask if sports really do contribute to the development of leaders.

The answer is "It depends." For sports champions and star individual contributors to move into the ranks of leadership, they need to perform a potentially unnatural act. They have to decide to get outside of themselves and focus on the success of others. "Athlete populations are me-centered," says Sharon Stoll, PhD, professor in the College of Education and director of the Center for Ethics at the University of Idaho, in describing how challenging this move can be. Given the amount of time and self-focus that is required to become a sports champion today, it is all too easy for a star to be self-absorbed to the point of narcissism. Dr. Stoll believes that more often than not, athletes are treated as though they are the center of the universe, which of course just reinforces their focus on themselves.

So it is the rare athlete and even the rarer champion who changes that focus and its underlying beliefs in order to become a leader. Failing to make the change, however, can have devastating consequences for champion athletes after their retirement. And the lessons apply just as readily for star individual contributors in business.

Steve Case—
Comeback Kid

America loves a comeback story. Steve Case spent 20 years building America Online into the world's dominant Internet powerhouse. In January 2001, at the pinnacle of the company's influence and market value, Case led what became the infamous AOL acquisition of Time Warner. He spent 2 years as chairman of the combined company, giving up that position in May 2003.

But it's now 2007 and Steve Case is back. Never one to be satisfied with the status quo, in April 2005, Case launched Revolution LLC, www.revolution.com, a private holding company that he has funded with $500 million of his estimated $825 million in wealth to invest in health care, wellness, and resorts—three sectors for which he sees significant sustained growth. Today, his company has about 2,500 employees across its three operating groups, Revolution Living, Revolution Resorts, and Revolution Health, and several hundred millions of dollars in revenues.

An innovator of the first order with a conviction about how to achieve positive impact on the world, Steve's leadership style is based on thinking big, change-the-world thoughts; playing to his strengths as a visionary evangelist for the consumer and deal maker; understanding how technology can serve people; and building a world-class team of colleagues, advisors, and managers to run the business operations.

"Revolution is building businesses that change the world," Case says. "We are focusing on major challenges that could be addressed through philanthropy, politics, or the public sector. But for me, given my interests and skills, I think I can have the greatest impact through an entrepreneurial prism, building on the AOL experience. At AOL, we were very mission driven. We really were motivated as much by getting people online and ushering in a more interactive age as we were about building a business and making money. That same philosophy applies particularly in areas like home health care, which is a broken system that demands a swing-for-the-fences kind of approach to empower consumers, leverage technology, and effect big change."

It is gratifying for Case to finally be able to live in the present and be forward-looking rather than defending the AOL–Time Warner merger. One lesson he says he learned: "I think I'm better at the earlier-stage ventures; I'm better playing offense than defense. When companies get large, they tend to focus as much on protecting what they have as building, and I'm much more a builder than a manager."

Three leadership lessons from Steve Case:

1. Learn from but don't dwell on past mistakes; have the courage to think great thoughts.

2. Be self-aware and objective about what you do well; surround yourself with people who complement your strengths and balance your weaknesses.

3. To create significant entrepreneurial and professional opportunities, understand and align yourself with major demographic, technological, and consumer preference trends, and take a long-term view.

DEVASTATING CONSEQUENCES

Why do top athletes have such a difficult time leaving their sport? Why did Michael Jordan, the greatest basketball player of all time, end his career and then return to the court not just once, but twice, even if the consequences for his legendary status were inevitably negative? Why did Mario Lemieux, one of the best hockey players in history, not retire earlier from the Pittsburgh Penguins, before his legions of fans had to compare the aging star with the memories of his former glory?

Many sports champions turn into waste once their careers are over. They careen off of The Dynamic Path and slide onto a different path altogether—that of the fallen champion. They no longer increase their level of greatness or positive impact on others and retract into shells of themselves. This phenomenon is caused, in part, by the removal of the structure that has guided their lives for many years. The irreversible physical damage that comes from years of punishing the body also takes its toll. The psychological damage, however, often overlooked, is just as significant. How do you make the smooth transition from demigod to a reasonably normal person? Jordan's and Lemieux's initial answer—trying to avoid the difficult transition by postponing it—is a recipe for physical and psychological deterioration. Babe Ruth followed this approach. After the New York Yankees, whose success and recognition he had almost single-handedly built, made it painfully clear by 1935 that they no longer needed his services, he joined the Boston Braves. His performance there became a depressing shadow of his once-glorious career. Ruth spent the final years of his life waiting for an offer from a major league team to become its manager. But the call never came.

Even the former champions who do become coaches, especially player-coaches like Jordan and Lemieux, are usually only disappointed in their new situation. Remaining a bit player in the environment they once dominated only makes it more painfully obvious how much of a civilian they have become. At the other end of the spectrum of trying to hang on is withdrawing from public life altogether. This was the course chosen by Joe DiMaggio, who dropped completely out of sight after his great career as a Yankee. He became invisible and spent his life away from the world, hidden behind financial managers who administered whatever assets were left from his public life.

The list of fallen champions, unfortunately, is very long. Dwight Gooden and Darryl Strawberry were superstars and celebrities on baseball's world-champion New York Mets 20 years ago. Likewise, Mike Tyson was the heavyweight boxing champion of the world. But like the mythological Icarus, who flew too close to the sun and melted his wings, they crashed. Each of these star athletes and many others like them seemingly had it all. But each of them lost it all. They let their egos get out of control, lost touch with reality, and developed an attitude of being above the law. This poisonous brew is not unique to athletes. Just think about the greedy, fraudulent business executives who are now wearing orange jumpsuits.

Within the safety of sports or at the top of a business, individuals can point toward concrete goals and push themselves to their limits, feeling the satisfaction of progress and achievement. But when it is time to go, it can be difficult for champion athletes and other top performers to sustain their greatness and continue to be successful. The most essential requirement for avoiding the fate of the fallen champion is to plan ahead and lay the groundwork early on for life on the other side of the current field of performance.

✦

Roger Staubach—
A Decade of Preparation

Perhaps the greatest transformation from legendary sports star to world-class business leader is Roger Staubach. In 1969, Staubach joined the Dallas Cowboys as a 27-year-old rookie, became the starting quarterback in his third season in 1971, and for the next nine seasons led "America's Team" with distinction. Staubach guided the Cowboys to six National Football Conference Championship Games, four Super Bowl appearances, and two NFL championships (winning Super Bowls VI and XII).

Staubach grew up in Cincinnati, Ohio, and won an appointment to the US Naval Academy, where he became arguably the best quarterback in the academy's history. He won the Heisman Trophy in 1963 during his junior year. Despite his success, he was not selected until the 10th round of the 1964 NFL draft. Most teams were scared off by Staubach's naval commitment, which required him to wait 5 years before breaking into the NFL. When he finally got his chance, he thrived, developing a reputation over his career for pulling memorable victories from the jaws of defeat. He led the Cowboys to 23 come-from-behind victories in the fourth quarter, 17 of which were in the final 2 minutes of the game. Staubach was inducted into the Pro Football Hall of Fame in 1985.

Beyond his distinguished football achievements, perhaps the most important thing Staubach did in his professional life—and the key lesson for champions seeking to transform themselves—is that he laid the groundwork for his post-football career *a decade* before he retired. "When I started playing pro football," Staubach says, "I knew that if I was injured, I was still going to be a young guy with a family to support. So, in 1970, I started working in the off-season for Henry S. Miller Company (the largest independent real estate brokerage firm in Texas, founded in 1914). I knew that if I just retired one day cold turkey, it would have been very difficult. It's hard to start over again, especially if you're an athlete." Henry S. Miller Jr., son of the company's founder and CEO of the firm, was Staubach's mentor. "He gave me a desk, a phone, and really taught me real estate," Staubach says.

Seven years of off-season work later and 2 years before his 1979 retirement from the Cowboys, he launched the Staubach Company, which today is a market-leading global real estate advisory firm with 1,200 employees in 58 offices representing 2,200 clients. The company now completes more than 5,000 transactions a year, with values approaching $20 billion.

"If I hadn't had those years in the trenches with the Miller Company, it would have been very difficult to transfer my 11 years in the NFL to starting over again in a business," Staubach says. "If athletes want to have a successful post-sports career today, they need to invest the time to transfer their experience from one business to another. That means that they've got to give up the golf tournaments and all the things that athletes can do in the off-season. Athlete or not, you still have to work in the trenches and persevere in order to succeed. No matter what you do in life, it's not going to happen easily, so you can't quit. You have to pay the price."

SELLING THE FAMILY SILVER

Bjorn Borg, one of the greatest tennis champions in history, sadly, never built on what he accomplished to achieve enduring greatness. To the disappointment of tennis fans around the world and to the veritable dismay of his foil John McEnroe, Borg retired from the game at age 27.

After McEnroe defeated him in the 1981 finals at Wimbledon and then again 2 months later at the US Open, Borg stopped playing major tournaments. Of this sudden move, McEnroe said, "To me it was devastating. I certainly got very empty after that because it had been so very exciting up to that point. Our personalities were so different, the way we played was so different, nothing ever needed to be said."

Other than serving as the consummate role model of focus and concentration, Borg was never really a leader of people. Nor did he take the opportunities that would have been afforded to him by his celebrity, access, and financial resources to create something greater than himself. In fact, a quarter-century after his Wimbledon heroics, Borg made an unprecedented announcement that he would sell the trophies from his record five consecutive Wimbledon titles by auction as well as two autographed Donnay racquets that he used in the finals, including in his epic 1980 victory over McEnroe. Unfortunately, it was not legacy building that led Borg to become the first player in history to sell Wimbledon hardware. Rather, he needed to raise money after a long series of bad business decisions led to serious financial trouble. While he obviously felt the need to build some financial security—the auctions were expected to generate about a half million dollars—I find it genuinely sad that he had to cling to his past greatness. "What I will always retain," Borg was quoted as saying in *Tennis* magazine, "is the knowledge that for such a long period of time, I was the supreme world tennis champion."

INDIVIDUALIZED DYNAMIC PATHS

To explore and contrast the differences between the legacy builder and the fallen champion, consider the chart on page 115, which takes some of the greatest names in the modern history of tennis and arrays them along individualized dynamic paths. Let's start with Roger Federer, who is quickly establishing himself as the greatest player of all time.

Right now he is at the pinnacle of his tennis career. And while he will almost certainly continue to rack up victories in the Grand Slam and regular Tour events, his natural physical talents will at some point inevitably wane, and his wins will become fewer and farther in between.

The questions for Federer, therefore, are: Where does he go from here? At what point does he start taking the next steps? How will he use his skills, access, and credibility to lay the foundation for his continued development, success, and impact after his professional career? And what aspirations will drive Federer forward to exercise the same passion off the court that he has on the court in the years to come?

Billie Jean King, John McEnroe, and Chris Evert have each built on their respective legendary successes in tennis to move into leadership and legacy-building positions, ranging from catalyzing girls' and women's sports, to establishing schools and training academies, to performing perhaps the sharpest sports commentary on television today. The nature of their work and contributions determine the shapes of their curves, and in particular, where along the admittedly subjective scale of greatness they fall. The arc of Arthur Ashe's brilliant career and inspiring life, for example, leads me to ascribe a Dynamic Path to him that has a shape different than the others. While he was a great tennis player, with his single Wimbledon and Australian and US Open victories, he did not achieve the greatness *as a tennis champion* of King, McEnroe, Evert, Borg, or Federer. However, based on his leadership work in civil rights and as an ambassador for tennis among other things, his enduring legacy approaches the import and impact of any tennis player or sports leader ever.

Finally, think about the shape of Bjorn Borg's Dynamic Path. As described above, he was not able to break through from one level to another after his great tennis career, and his curve unfortunately took a nosedive sometime after his early retirement.

Tennis Greats and Their Dynamic Paths

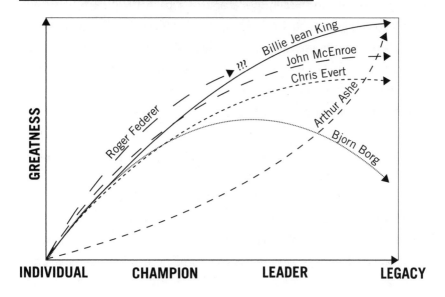

The Reinvention
of Terry Bradshaw

Talk about a dynamic path. Growing up in the impoverished rural South and achieving greatness as a Hall of Fame NFL quarterback, Terry Bradshaw has transformed himself into a one-man multimedia empire.

Born September 2, 1948, in Shreveport, Louisiana, Bradshaw went from Woodlawn High School to Louisiana Tech, where he still holds the single-season passing and total offense records. Bradshaw was one of the most prolific quarter-backs in history, leading the Pittsburgh Steelers to four Super Bowl champion-ships, six American Football Conference championship games, and eight straight play-off appearances from 1972 to 1979. Like other great champions, he thrived when it counted most: in winner-take-all postseason games. Under his leadership, the Steelers won Super Bowl championships in 1975, 1976, 1979, and 1980, giving him a perfect 4-0 record in Super Bowl play. "My strength was performing under pressure," Bradshaw says, "and it always has been. From high school I always performed in the big games; I always delivered, in college and in the pros." Five years after the close of his 14-year NFL career, he was inducted into the Pro Football Hall of Fame in 1989, his first year of eligibility.

In the more than 2 decades since his 1984 retirement, Bradshaw has reinvented himself as an Emmy Award–winning broadcaster, a gold-record-level recording artist, a best-selling author, and a star actor.

Along with broadcast and video game star John Madden, Bradshaw is widely acknowledged as today's preeminent NFL studio personality. He serves the dual role of cohost and analyst on *Fox NFL Sunday.* The show is America's most-watched NFL pregame show—a feat recognized by four Emmy Awards. Bradshaw launched his broadcasting career by joining CBS Sports as an NFL game analyst right after leaving the field. He learned the broadcasting business with the same fierce determination that described his work ethic on the field. He served in almost every conceivable on-air role, from game analyst to studio analyst to play-by-play announcer, to contributor on *The Super Bowl Today* programs, to pregame, half-time, and postgame commentator. He is known for his hyperactive energy, quick wit, and sharp insights into the minds of the players on the field.

Beyond his television broadcasting career, Bradshaw has appeared in several feature films and guest-starred on several television series. He has also written five books and is a widely sought-after motivational speaker, ranked at the upper echelons of the genre.

Bradshaw's reinvention came about by necessity. "The funny thing about a professional athlete," he says, "is that we spend all our time honing in on our craft because we want to get to the big show. And you work, and work, and work, and work. But when you finally get to the big show, you can only be there for such a small period of time. After you get out, you have at least a third of your productive life remaining, so you've got to do something else."

For Bradshaw, his transition from the Steelers was made more difficult by getting into a tiff with head coach Chuck Noll and the Pittsburgh community on his way out. "I got hurt and tried to play, and I ended up finishing off my career with a torn ligament in my elbow. I was mad that I had to retire, and I felt I deserved a little bit more respect from my head coach." What ensued was a long period when Bradshaw did not visit or associate with Pittsburgh. The fans felt cheated out of the greatest period in the franchise's history. "I have grown up since then," Bradshaw says, "and took it upon myself to say that it was my own immaturity that led to leaving on such strained terms. So I've admitted guilt. I've apologized and patched things up with the city. I thought it was important to bend over backwards. And now it's all good."

When a leader comes forth and opens up as such, people usually come back in support even more strongly. "When you're honest with people, when you say, 'I made a mistake, you're right,' you build an amazing bond.

"We grew up poor," Bradshaw says, "and the one thing that kept everybody grounded, the thing that everybody's happiness revolved around was the family, when everybody was together." That's where his values hail from. His family learned to make their own fun. "We used to pitch washers at holes in the ground. We used to go coon hunting. We'd build paper kites and use sticks out of the field and make our own paste. And we used to dig holes in the banks of the dirt and put a chimney in it and use that to cook marshmallows. We made up our own toys and created our own entertainment. We never thought, 'Well, we don't have money.' We never thought that we needed this or that. Everybody just seemed to be happy being together as a family, playing cards and dominos, cooking and barbecuing.

"When I discovered football, it stayed with me all day long. If I wasn't playing and practicing, I was on the field afterward, throwing. I was at home throwing, all summer long throwing. When I was a little boy, I was always throwing, always looking for somebody to catch it. I was just absolutely fascinated with throwing the football; I never could do it enough. I used to throw it at the old swing set and roll out pretending I was Bart Starr or Johnny Unitas. And I dreamed of being in the NFL one day."

117

Even with an imagination free from the electronics and media cluttering the minds of today's young people, I'm sure Bradshaw couldn't possibly have dreamed of accomplishing all that he has over his remarkable and still-evolving career. The most important lesson that Bradshaw took from football to life after the field is the importance of hard work, commitment, and passion. "You need to apply passion to everything you do. If you don't have the passion, you're not successful and you'll just go on bitchin'. Without the passion there won't be commitment, and without commitment there won't be success."

THE CHALLENGES AND RISKS OF LEAVING YOUR PERCH

For people in business, the challenges and perils of leaving your championship perch are also epic. The individual performer in business has no more difficult a transition in front of him. After working over a period of years to become a highly valued (and potentially highly compensated) individual contributor, it is exceedingly difficult to change and break through to become a leader.

This is perhaps the most important and perilous dynamic moment, when you have to progress from an individual competitor to a leader. What difficulties make this moment so perilous? First, it requires fundamental changes in your mindset as well as your actions. Secondly, there are powerful pressures *against* this change. And thirdly, there are very real risks associated with it. Confronting the need to make such a change is inevitable. I've heard it said many times that "[fill in the blank] is a young person's business." Wall Street, advertising, consulting, retail, high tech, and others—each has been described as a young person's business. You can embrace the need to change, ignore it, or run the other way. But there will come a time when you will no longer be able to stay in the same game and rely on the talents and hard work that got you to where you are.

Whether you are a rainmaking sales executive, a money-minting trader, an award-winning designer, a name-brand architect, a page-one journalist, or a highly sought-after lawyer, it takes years of dedication and hard work to transform your natural talents—your potential value— into the experience, reputation, and expertise—your experiential value— to get to the top of your field. The transition to leader of others is so difficult because the skills that got you to be a champion in the first place are likely to be highly specialized and not necessarily transferable. Making judgments about people, setting performance targets, holding people accountable, developing and managing budgets, running good meetings, establishing efficient management processes—this is the stuff that leading others effectively is all about. Those are not the skills needed by the star individual. In light of that, it is not at all surprising that top individual contributors often don't make the best managers, and this fact is widely known in management circles.

But if the difficulties are so well known, why do the top individual practitioners so often get the nod? For one thing, there is frequently an assumption that if you are successful at one thing, you will be successful at the next. Others may believe in you and your potential to develop the necessary skills. Credibility is also always a central consideration. It is difficult for other star individuals to accept someone into a leadership position who has not been a successful individual performer himself. Finally, decision makers may calculate that the risk of you not develop- ing the requisite skills is smaller than the risk of bringing in someone with management experience but who lacks the personal-performance track record.

The pressure against making the change from individual to leader is based on the fact that it often goes against the grain of your ego. When you are the rainmaker or champion, you get enormous attention and continuous feedback as a result of your exploits and efforts. You are the one "paying the bills around here." People want to keep you happy and support you. It's natural in this situation for others to feed your ego and tell you how great you are. After all, what you are doing has value for them; they don't want to lose you as a source of revenue or recognition.

It takes mental toughness to avoid thinking that what you do is the result of some brilliant plan or that your skill or success means that you are a fundamentally good person. Remember the truth about winning? Just as making mistakes on the tennis court or losing a golf match has no bearing on your quality as a person, so too is the case in reverse. Your success per se in and of itself has little bearing on your quality as a person.

It can be financially risky to move from individual to leader. Oftentimes, the top bankers, salespeople, traders, designers, or "talent" are the most highly compensated in an organization. It is they who are building the franchise, generating the revenue, and creating opportunities for others. When you move from the front lines of creating the value to leading other people who are doing so, it is not unusual to have to take a step backward in income.

With all the risks, pressures, and disincentives financially, why attempt to transition at all? For this reason: Doing so will force you to keep growing by stretching and challenging yourself. Only by continuing to grow can you reap the full benefits of the harvest phase of your career and avoid The Fallen Champion's Path. Doing so will also allow you to continue traveling along The Dynamic Path and make an enduring contribution.

To maximize the likelihood of your continued success, you need to move to the next stage of The Dynamic Path and become a great leader. Some straightforward principles will guide you along the way: Accept and embrace the fact that you have to change from being an individual contributor to working with and through others. Focus on the success of others who work with and for you. The more successful you enable them to become, the more they will in turn do everything they can to make you a success. And be a good listener, avoiding the temptation to be a know-it-all.

Let's now move ahead and visit with some of the individuals who did all this and more, so we can discover how they have become great leaders and how their lessons can accelerate your own progression along The Dynamic Path.

CHAPTER 7

The Making of
a Great Leader

There they were, sitting proudly upon the mantel: the Claret Jug from the British Open and the US Amateur and US Open championship trophies. On the wall to the right of the fireplace, photographs hung of a dapper man with a charming smile playing golf with Republican presidents. There he was with wavy brown hair alongside Dwight D. Eisenhower and again with Richard M. Nixon and twice more with Gerald Ford. There he was, now with salt-and-pepper locks, beside Ronald Reagan and later with George H.W. Bush. Most recently, there he was again, this time with distinguished white hair, with George W. Bush. A picture of the same man teeing it up with Bill Clinton at the 1996 Presidents Cup hangs (not coincidentally) to the left of the fireplace. There are photos with Queen Elizabeth at a White House reception, half a dozen letters received from presidents, and his favorite, a note from President Eisenhower settling a $10 bet.

The Presidential Medal of Freedom, the highest honor bestowed on a US civilian by the White House, is displayed nobly behind a glass case. Directly across the room, on a four-sided bookcase that rotates manually, sits a silver replica of the fabled square clubhouse of Augusta National, with engravings celebrating Masters victories in 1958, 1960, 1962, and 1964.

This was the house that Arnie built.

ARNOLD PALMER COUNTRY

Nestled in the foothills of the Allegheny Mountains some 35 miles east of Pittsburgh, Latrobe, Pennsylvania, is the heart of Arnold Palmer country. Northwest Airlines flights buzz in and out of Arnold Palmer Regional Airport, which sits just 1 mile up Arnold Palmer Drive from the modest one-story home in which Palmer grew up. His Latrobe Country Club, where he learned to play from his father, Milfred "Deacon" Palmer, who was first the greenskeeper and later rose to become the club's teaching professional as well, sits right across the entrance to Legends Lane. Up at the end of that hilly lane stands one of Palmer's homes and one set of offices from which his multinational business and philanthropic enterprise is run.

Palmer country extends well beyond Latrobe, first to the Arnold Palmer Pavilion, a core part of the Excela Health hospital complex, a joint venture with the University of Pittsburgh Medical Center that provides state-of-the-art radiation and chemotherapy treatment for cancer patients. It continues on to central Florida, where Palmer's Bay Hill Club and residential community are based and where he hosts the annual Arnold Palmer Invitational golf tournament for the PGA Tour. Nearby in Orlando sits the Arnold Palmer Medical Center, which incorporates the Arnold Palmer Hospital for Children and the Winnie Palmer Hospital for Women & Babies. Palmer and his company have contributed more than $50 million to make this hospital and its world-class trauma center for children a reality.

Palmer country radiates still farther, all across the world, on the shoulders of "Arnie's Army." The so-called largest nonuniformed military organization in existence, informally formed at the 1960 Masters, consists of thousands of die-hard Palmer fans, who like millions of others around the world have made him one of the most popular and accessible sports figures in history.

Palmer's golf exploits need little mentioning: 61 PGA Tour victories, including seven major championships, 19 international professional tournament wins, and 12 Senior PGA Tour (now called Champions

Tour) championships, for a total of 92 wins. Palmer's most prolific years were 1960 to 1963, when he won 29 PGA Tour events in four seasons. In 1960, he was named *Sports Illustrated* magazine's "Sportsman of the Year," and in 1967, he became the first man to reach one million dollars in career earnings on the PGA Tour. His overall earnings on the Tour totaled $6.9 million.

Arnold Palmer isn't the best player in the history of men's professional golf, nor even close to the leading money winners of more recent times. Yet he was the sport's most important trailblazer and, until Tiger Woods, arguably golf's most popular star. Palmer's dynamism was an important factor in establishing golf as a compelling event for television in the 1950s and 1960s, and in so doing he established the foundation for its popularity today. The characteristics that made Palmer the first star in the sport's television age were his boyishly handsome looks, his humble family background, the way he took risks at key moments in big tournaments, his string of exciting finishes in early televised tournaments, and his charismatic personality.

Palmer's magnetism endures to this day. I saw him at the 2006 Masters, wearing the signature green blazer of Augusta National members and past champions, attracting throngs of fans who swarmed to see him up close, shake his hand, and wish him well. His engaging interactions are not unlike those of former President Bill Clinton in the way he relates to individuals, drawing on their energy and turning it right back to them in an amplified way. Even over the course of only a moment, people feel as if they have a genuine connection with Arnold Palmer.

Palmer was a champion on the golf course in the United States, in Great Britain (where he almost single-handedly made the British Open a must-play event for American golfers), and all around the world. Although his career in professional golf was notable, it is what Palmer has done with his golf, and all that was made possible as a result, that has made him a great leader.

SPORTS MARKETING PIONEER

Palmer laid the foundation for his leadership during the height of his professional success. He was the first client of Mark McCormack, an enterprising attorney from Cleveland who pioneered the business of representing and managing talent. McCormack, who went on to create sports marketing behemoth International Management Group, or IMG, helped establish Arnold Palmer Enterprises, a multidivision structure encompassing a broad range of businesses. Palmer has been active in licensing, endorsements, and as a spokesman for some of the world's leading brands. He also has a wide range of golf-related activities. These include the Arnold Palmer Design Company, which since the mid-1960s has allowed him to put his mark on more than 200 new courses throughout the world; the Arnold Palmer Golf Academy, which has a proprietary methodology for teaching high-performance golf; and Palmer-designed and branded sporting goods and golf equipment.

He also owns and is president of the Latrobe Country Club, which he acquired in 1971. When I visited the clubhouse, my immediate thought was that Palmer needed the country club simply to house and display the hundreds of plaques, trophies, honors, vintage collectibles, and other memorabilia he has collected during half a century of a preeminent golf, business, and public service career.

THE GOLF CHANNEL AND PGA TOUR

Within the world of golf, however, Palmer says that there are two other accomplishments of which he is proudest. One is his role as cofounder of The Golf Channel. In 1991, media entrepreneur Joseph E. Gibbs of Birmingham, Alabama, had a belief that sufficient interest existed among the public to support a 24-hour cable golf channel. After a Gallup survey confirmed the strong demand, Gibbs teamed up with Palmer to cofound The Golf Channel. With Palmer's imprimatur and active engagement in the programming concept, they were able to secure an initial investment from a consortium of six cable operators: Continental Cablevision, Comcast Cable Communications, Newhouse Broadcasting, Cablevision Industries, Adelphia Communications, and Times Mirror Company. More than $80 million was secured to finance the business.

This investment is an example of the key lesson taught in the entrepreneurial finance class that I took at Harvard Business School in 1985. Professor Bill Sahlman, a legend in the venture capital world, taught that in entrepreneurship, "the *who* is more important than the *what*." That is, who you get to invest in your venture is more important than how much they invest or even the financial terms. In this case, by making an investment in The Golf Channel, the cable companies not only provided the necessary capital, they ensured distribution for The Golf Channel on their cable systems. This in turn enabled and legitimized the network as a viable business.

The Golf Channel went live on January 19, 1995, televising its first tournament, the Dubai Desert Classic. Today, the network is available in more than 90 million homes worldwide, and it broadcasts more live golf coverage than any other network. Without Arnold Palmer's active leadership in the planning, launch, and growth of The Golf Channel, the company would not be in existence today.

The second enduring golf-related legacy for which Palmer is most proud is his central role in the establishment of the modern PGA Tour. The history of the Tour traces its roots back to 1895, when 10 professional golfers and one amateur played in the first US Open in Newport, Rhode Island. This was followed shortly thereafter by tournaments sprouting up all across the country. But there was no continuity or consistency among the events. The first "playing pros" organization was formed in 1932, and the sport became more structured following World War II. In the late 1950s and early 1960s, interest in golf exploded when Palmer's telegenics and President Eisenhower's passion for the game inspired millions to give it a try. Palmer says that the formal beginning of the PGA Tour was in late 1968, when the Tournament Players Division split from the PGA of America. "We wanted to capitalize on the sport's interest and commercial potential by all coming together in a professionally managed league operation," he notes. Palmer was instrumental in persuading the other leading players to get behind the concept, and he played a key role in hiring Joseph C. Dey as the Tour's first commissioner.

ARNIE AS ROLE MODEL

This chapter is concerned with the makings of a great leader, of which Palmer is a prime example. However, he has also moved into the realm of legacy builder with his long and deep commitment to battling cancer and improving health care. This is an important part of his life given that he lost his first wife, Winnie, to the disease, and that he successfully battled prostate cancer.

What is it about Arnold Palmer that makes him so magnetic and such a role model? For one thing, he genuinely cares about other people. You can't fake this. Palmer takes energy from others and transmits positive energy back to them. He also concentrates on only a few priorities and attracts outstanding people to help get them accomplished. Contracting with Mark McCormack, for example, was a shrewd decision that over 4 decades generated the necessary financial resources and organizational infrastructure to get things done. The nature of his contract with McCormack also says volumes about his integrity, which is the essential and fundamental base ingredient of leadership. There was never any written contract between Palmer and McCormack. The building of a multimillion-dollar enterprise and the foundation of the entire sports marketing industry were based on a legendary handshake in 1960.

LEADERSHIP: A SURPRISING WAY TO SUCCEED

Leadership is such a popular topic that people sometimes forget why it's so important in the first place. Psychologists are convinced that over the long term, people act only in their self-interest. That is, they will sustain a set of behaviors only if they believe that it will serve or reinforce their own interests. Leadership and success, it turns out, go hand in hand, which explains why people give the subject so much attention.

If you want a fail-safe way to be successful, don't worry about your own short-term success. Dedicate yourself to making *those around you* successful. As mentioned in Chapter 2, my research found that among the most successful business leaders, the vast majority are described as "caring as much about the success of those who work with and for them as their own success," whereas only a small percentage are described as putting their own success ahead of that of their peers and subordinates. Of course, lest you think that you can be incompetent and still care only about the success of others, it is safe to presume that those in the population studied are all somewhere between effective and excellent at the fundamentals of their jobs.

Think about the power of this notion. Focusing on the success of others will lead directly to your own success. While this may not be the quickest path to success, it works. It works because by doing so, you attract the very best people to work with you. All the energy that you dedicate to their success rebounds to you as they, in turn, become committed to your success.

To the hundreds of CEOs and top executives with whom I work, this may not seem surprising. But to most employees within organizations obsessed with quarterly results, nothing could be more counterintuitive. Fifteen years of globalization, hyper-competition, reengineering, downsizing, and layoff after painful layoff has produced a cynical workforce that believes only in survival of the fittest—i.e., if you win, I lose.

The belief that progressing through your career requires competing against colleagues rather than supporting them is one of the most pervasive misconceptions in the workplace today. Not only is it dangerous—stifling productivity and spawning behavior inconsistent with the core values of ethics and integrity—it is most assuredly not the way to pursue The Dynamic Path. Yes, this requires a shift from the hyper-competitive mindset of the top champion or individual contributor at work. But leadership is no longer about winning individually. It is about enabling the team or organization to win.

TONY HAWK: SKATEBOARD KING AND COMMUNITY LEADER

About 5 years ago, I watched as my sons Teddy and Oliver were playing a video game and guiding a cool-looking character through cityscapes and beachfront skateparks. "Who's that?" I asked innocently. The boys, then 12 and 10, looked at me as if I was from Mars. That was my first exposure to Tony Hawk.

Ask any teenager about Tony Hawk, and they'll give you that same look. Now approaching 40 years old, Hawk is one of the heroes of America's youth and reportedly the second-most-visible athlete in the United States after Tiger Woods. With all that he has accomplished as an athlete, a business leader, and a philanthropist, Hawk has grown from individual to champion and from champion to leader. While he is now at the height of his leadership, he is well on his way to building an enduring legacy.

Tony Hawk became the world's best skateboarder by applying his natural talents, unrelenting dedication, a ferocious zeal to succeed, and a history of overcoming life obstacles. Hawk innovated constantly, pushing the envelope of what could be done on a skateboard, inventing many moves such as the "Ollie 540," the "Kickflip 540," and the "Varial 720."

His greatest move was landing the first-ever "900" (two and a half mid-air spins) at the 1999 X Games. He built on his skateboarding successes, launching different lines of businesses, including boards, shoes, a clothing brand, and most importantly, video games. In 1999, Activision and he created "Tony Hawk's Pro Skater" video game for Sony PlayStation. They expected solid sales, but it quickly became a blockbuster. Since then, the THPS series has become one of the best-selling video-game franchises of all time, with sales totaling $1.1 billion. With Hawk's commercial success, he further broadened his offerings to include a direct-to-DVD movie, *Boom Boom Sabotage*, a weekly satellite radio show on Sirius, Hawk-inspired cell-phone ringtones, and the soon-to-be-launched "Tony Hawk Experience" at Six Flags theme parks. Now a father of three and moving into middle age, Hawk has maintained his connection to America's fickle youth, managing to remain cool and relevant and allowing him to generate $5 million to $7 million a year from his commercial activities.

Here is where Hawk has stepped up beyond athlete-turned-business-mogul to move to a greater level of leadership. In 2002, he founded the Tony Hawk Foundation to give back to the sport that has given him so much. The foundation provides grants to communities so they can build skateparks to provide a place for young people to be outdoors skating, getting exercise, and being with others. The foundation focuses particularly on low-income areas that have a high percentage of at-risk youth, *and* whose communities demonstrate a strong grassroots commitment to the project. Over the past 5 years, the foundation has awarded grants ranging from $5,000 to $25,000 to 273 communities around the United States for an aggregate gift of $1,167,000. The awards and the community involvement that they have stimulated have impacted the lives of tens of thousands of young people who otherwise would not have those resources available.

FROM HOUSEHOLD TERROR
TO WORLD CHAMPION

From Hawk's early days as a relatively normal kid, he soon developed many of the patterns of a champion. As a boy growing up in Southern California, Hawk says, "I played all the traditional sports—hockey, football, and basketball. I had a good time playing these sports with my friends, but I was never deeply interested in them, even though I wanted to be." He was also a self-proclaimed terror around the house. "I was terrible," Hawk says, "aggravated and hyper." His frustration was so harsh that his parents had him evaluated at school. The good news was that they found he didn't have any learning disabilities at all; in fact, he was gifted, with the mind of a 12-year-old. The bad news was that this active and intelligent mind was trapped inside the body of an 8-year-old, preventing him from accomplishing what his brain thought his body should be able to do. This all started to change when he turned 9 years old and his brother gave him a blue fiberglass banana skateboard.

It turned out to be a gift that would change his life.

"When I finally started skating," Hawk explains, "I really liked it because I didn't have a coach yelling at me or telling me where to go. I didn't have to show up at a practice at a certain time. It was all about my own motivation and my own challenges." Contrary to popular belief, Hawk wasn't an immediate natural on the board in those early days. He was skating and learning just like his friends. "I was actually intimidated and nervous. But at the same time, I was excited," he says. "It was also hard, for sure. But I felt like I was in my own space." He didn't realize it at the time, but as he grew older and got better, there was always something new to learn. "No matter how far you get in skating, you can always push it that much more—an entirely new trick or a variation on an existing trick. I felt like it was limitless."

Hawk went into competitions a year later. His father, an enthusiastic supporter of his skateboarding, happily drove him and his friends to the local competitions around their Los Angeles suburb of Belmar. Very soon he was carting them to tournaments all across Southern California. Hawk loved the sport, practiced it endlessly, and thrived. By the time he was 14, he was doing extraordinarily well competitively and had gotten noticed by skateboard manufacturers. He decided it was time to turn pro. While this may sound grandiose, it wasn't a very big deal, says Hawk, given the early state of development of the sport at the time. "It was my hobby, what I loved doing. Basically, you had to check a box on the entry form, and one said pro and the other amateur. There wasn't some courting by a sponsor or grooming to come into the professional field. It was more like, 'Well, you've reached the top of the amateur ranks, you can now check the pro box,' and that was it." There were only about 50 professional skaters at the time competing for first place prizes worth a startling $200.

So, it wasn't the money that motivated Hawk to dedicate himself to skating. It was his passion. Hawk became renowned for inventing new moves. His training regimen was focused on learning the skills that he hadn't yet mastered and then coming up with others that had never before been done. As the saying goes, necessity is the mother of invention. Hawk was so small that he was constantly searching for ways to keep up his speed to get the necessary height to do the new tricks. "To do some of the spinning moves where you're flipping your board around," Hawk says, "you have to get plenty of air time to maneuver the board and get it back under your feet. One of my biggest challenges was figuring out how to propel myself to get that speed, because I was so much smaller than everyone else." To accomplish that, he invented a new technique that today is the standard for the sport. "Rather than reaching down and grabbing the skateboard before you leave the lip of the ramp, I was able actually to launch into the air just using my speed and then grab the board at the apex of the turn. I was ridiculed for it in those days because people said that I was cheating. But as long as you were already into a move and just touched it, you were allowed to do it."

As time went on, people realized that this was the only way to get a lot of height. "Once you reach around and grab your board before you leave the lip of the ramp, half of the speed you've generated has been nullified because you've reached air and your legs have stopped propelling you," Hawk explains.

His hard work, dedication, and innovation paid off handsomely. By age 16, Hawk was the best skateboarder in the world. Over the ensuing 17 years until his retirement from competition in 2001, Hawk competed in an estimated 103 pro contests, won 73 of them, and placed second in another 19. This is the best record in skateboarding's history, by far.

In 2002, Hawk launched the Boom Boom HuckJam, a 30-city arena extreme-sports spectacular featuring the world's best skateboarders, BMX bike riders, and motocross daredevils performing choreographed routines on million-dollar ramp systems, set to blaring hip-hop music. The hugely successful HuckJam tour, in which Hawk himself continues to perform, has sold out arenas across the country every year since its inception.

TONY HAWK TODAY

Today, Tony Hawk is one part business leader and one part community leader. His challenge is to maintain his success on the business side and to continue evolving on the community side. Hawk also has to continue to build his brand and the financial returns that go along with that while avoiding business deals that will cause his youth audience to think that he has sold out to the establishment. That's why no one should expect to see him sporting the Nike swoosh anytime soon. What we can expect is that he will continue to live the iconoclast lifestyle that young people find so compelling, while appealing to the parents of his teen and pre-teen fans by maintaining a clean-cut style, avoiding tattoos and body piercings, and always wearing a helmet.

Hawk is also obsessively hands-on when it comes to the programming of the THPS video games to ensure that every detail is accurate with regard to how skating is really done. "I grew up skateboarding," Hawk explains, "and I also grew up playing video games. So I am very discerning about both. I didn't want the games to have some ridiculous element that wasn't real in skating, just to try to get nonskaters into the game."

Authenticity, in fact, is one of Hawk's consistent themes. "We have a lot of people that like our brand because of who we are. We're skaters," Hawk says. "It's a skate brand made by a skater, so there's a legitimacy there. And we've been around since 1992. It's not like we suddenly saw that skating is big and decided to jump into the game."

Another priority has been to leverage the Tony Hawk brand and its promotional power to create a positive impact on the sport of skateboarding and its constituents. "A lot of times, especially with larger corporate sponsors," Hawk says, "I want to use the marketing dollars that they've agreed to assign to me to promote skating. So if they're going to show skating in a commercial, I want it to be the absolute best to inspire kids to get out there and skate, not just use skating because it's hot. Another requirement of a big sponsorship is to have them donate money to the foundation. So, I'm able to use McDonald's marketing dollars, for example, to build public skateparks."

Going back to his foundation, it is clear that the impetus for its establishment was based on a genuine desire to help others, not the self-promotional behavior of a superficial do-gooder. "The Tony Hawk Foundation mostly came about because as skating grew," Hawk says, "I attended some grand openings of public skateparks that a number of cities were building. The parks were terrible. They were embarrassing." It turns out that a lot of money had been spent and space assigned to create subpar parks, the result of which was that the kids thought that a small parking lot was a better place than the parks to skate. "I realized that a bad cycle was happening," Hawk continues, "where a city decided to fund a skatepark and then went out to get bids, and then the lowest sidewalk contractor threw in a bid saying they had experience. Then they didn't consult the skaters on the design of the place and didn't take into consideration the functionality of the park. They just interpreted what they'd seen on television or in the video games and said that they knew how to build a skatepark."

Hawk wanted to stop that cycle by empowering the people who were rallying for the skatepark in the first place. "We wanted to give funding to those who were trying to raise money to build a park in the first place, but we also wanted to give them the resources to do it properly. We also put a stipulation on the project saying that if they didn't follow certain guidelines, we weren't going to provide funding or our endorsement. We think our guidelines and endorsement hold a lot more importance than our financial grants since they are not large enough to build an entire skatepark. The people will submit a plan to us, and I will take it and literally write out suggestions by hand—'Put a rail here, face this ramp the other way'—no matter how small a recommendation. The goal is to make the parks much more skateable on the one hand and to empower communities with low-income areas and high-risk kids on the other hand."

LEARNING LEADERSHIP

A timeless question about leadership is whether leaders are born or bred. My belief, based on more than a decade of research and even longer as a student of the subject, leads me to conclude that leadership can, in fact, be learned. Of course, certain people are born with the natural charisma gene, the magnetism that attracts people from the earliest days on the playground and often runs all the way to the boardroom. But some of the most charismatic, attractive people go awry and self-destruct, while many of the quieter individuals end up having the greatest success in the most important leadership positions. This is because there are as many different styles of leadership as there are people, and the style is often situational. However, regardless of fashion, the underlying principles of leadership are eternal.

Bill Gates, for example, has a famously intense, analytical style that may not have worked if he were CEO of Costco, Starbucks, or Washington Mutual, or head coach of the Seattle Seahawks or Supersonics. But his style was obviously well suited for building the world's greatest software company in the same city as all of those organizations. What are the key elements of Gates's leadership? He had a superior original vision of how software could enable a computer to accomplish useful tasks; he built a superb management team; he and the team adapted to dramatic changes in technological capabilities, business needs, and the competitive environment; and they created a culture of excellence, dedication, and winning. That's leadership.

THE MAKING OF A GREAT LEADER

Let's take a look at the components of leadership as depicted by The Dynamic Path. The great leader is equal parts work ethic, problem solving, and people leadership. The "Composition of a Leader" chart on page 138 illustrates that work ethic and problem solving/mental toughness remain consistently important as you evolve from champion—or star individual contributor—to leader. Great leaders work as hard, are as dedicated, and are as mentally tough—finding the right solutions to the most important issues at the right moments in time—as champion individual contributors. In sports, the best coaches work as hard as, although less physically than, their top players. In business, the best business leaders work as hard as, although differently from, their best employees.

The dynamics involved in the making of a leader are threefold. First, success at this stage is less about your natural talent, because as a leader, it is less about you and more about taking responsibility for and inspiring others. So the area in the natural talent stratum declines as you move up The Dynamic Path. Secondly, people leadership is, by contrast, at its apex at the point when you become a great leader. Thirdly, as you become an ever stronger leader of people, one element that plays an increasingly important role is the exercise of moral and spiritual leadership. This is about living with integrity and leading by example; about standing for something fundamentally important and directing your attention and energies, and those of others, to making a positive impact on a few concentrated and important priorities.

In the remainder of this chapter, I will delve more deeply into what it really means to be a great leader and proffer some tangible advice on how to move closer to this virtuous state.

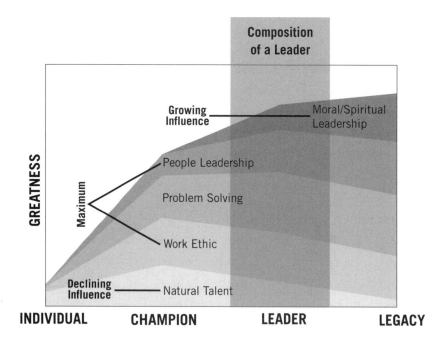

A GREAT LEADER IS A "BENEVOLENT" LEADER

THE BENEVOLENT LEADER—FOCUSED ON THE SUCCESS OF
OTHERS, AN OPEN AND HONEST LEADERSHIP STYLE BASED ON
TRUST, BROAD DELEGATION OF CRITICAL OBJECTIVES, AND
ALIGNMENT OF ORGANIZATIONAL AND INDIVIDUAL GOALS.

Benevolent leadership is an approach based on ultimate trust and the alignment of individual and organizational goals. As a leader, your ability to create a positive working environment, inspiring and galvanizing a loyal team of professionals working toward common success, is the most powerful way to ensure the success of your organization and yourself. This is what the people leadership layer on The Dynamic Path is all about. In short, the best way to think about how to maximize the people leadership component of The Dynamic Path is to focus continually on how to make *those around you* successful.

What are the attributes of the benevolent leader? He or she creates an environment of open communication, honesty, and confidence, delegating—but not abdicating—both minor and critical tasks. A benevolent leader demonstrates how the success of the team directly benefits each team member.

People long to work in an environment where bold aspirations for success are clearly defined and commonly shared and team behavior is governed by a strong set of ethics and core values. When the leader's attention is focused squarely on the success of team members, strong results, organizational performance, and employee loyalty are achieved naturally.

The best leaders maximize performance through facilitation. They eliminate barriers for subordinates and lead with authority, even though at times they appear to be just one of the pack. It's easy to know when a benevolent leader is in charge. The telltale signs: Information and authority flow freely, honesty abounds. People feel free to question authority without retribution. Creativity is celebrated. Each member of the team feels accountable to one another as well as to the leader.

What is it about the benevolent style of leadership that makes it so related to success? The answer lies in the environment that this creates within an organization and the effect that this has on the performance of team members. Benevolent leaders are advantaged by creating an environment where the very best performers want to work, will perform at peak levels, and will remain loyal. In turn, these leaders are rewarded by the excellent performance of those working with them.

What really motivates the best and brightest people? In earlier research, a colleague and I sought to identify how top-performing people in business defined career success. The most important factor was "freedom in my job to do the things I think are important." High-performing professionals do not like to be micromanaged. In truth, they don't really like to be managed at all. They prefer to be led with a clear set of goals and the creative freedom to accomplish their objectives the best way they see fit. They want to be trusted with the information and resources necessary to achieve a task and then be given the accountability, authority, and flexibility to do what's necessary. Strong players feel smothered by managers who are afraid to truly delegate responsibility or who view information as power. A high degree of trust and freedom is a core element of the most dynamic and desirable professional environments.

When they create this type of environment, benevolent leaders find themselves at a significant advantage because they consistently have their pick of the most talented people. This is where sports and business operate on the same plane. In sports, competition for star performers is intense—

whether at the college or professional level—and the schools or teams that have the best programs consistently recruit the best players. The result is usually that the schools or teams where athletes believe they are most likely to win keep on winning. Like athletes, business professionals understand the importance of joining the best company and actively seek it out. This becomes a virtuous circle—the best people create the best results, which in turn attract the best people. The ability to create the most attractive environment, therefore, pays tremendous dividends. As a leader, if you can create a winning environment, your team and you will end up a winner.

Marvin Lewis—
Taking the Cincinnati Bengals to a Higher Place

When Marvin Lewis showed up, the Cincinnati Bengals were in trouble. Since Lewis assumed the head coaching job, the team has turned into a playoff contender while attracting fan support and regular-season attendance in record numbers. In his rookie head coaching season of 2003, Cincinnati was the NFL's most improved team. Lewis is the only coach in the team's history never to post a losing season. While bringing the team more confidence and unity, he has also worked hard to strengthen the team's relations with the Cincinnati community, making more than 100 appearances in his first 2 years. When he was hired, Lewis became only the eighth African American to be named to an NFL head coaching position.

Born September 23, 1958, Lewis attended Fort Cherry High School in the town of McDonald in western Pennsylvania, a hotbed of football greatness. An all-conference quarterback and safety, he also earned high school letters in wrestling and baseball. Foretelling the future perhaps, Lewis went on to play football for Idaho State's team, the Bengals. While he was recruited to play quarterback, he ended up spending more time on defense. Lewis earned all–Big Sky Conference honors as an outside linebacker for ISU in 3 consecutive years, but, he says, "we didn't win a lot of football games. Fortunately, I had good coaches who taught me about the game. Even more importantly, they really showed me how to treat people and how to communicate well." That combination is what attracted Lewis to pursue coaching, which he did in 1981 at his alma mater, while earning his master's degree in athletic administration.

Lewis is cut from a different cloth than those from the Vince Lombardi or Bear Bryant school of coaching. When you watch Lewis work on the sidelines or conduct postgame interviews, he is much more connected to his players than those head coaches whose commanding style and remoteness from the players resembled World War II army generals. "I don't have that aura," Lewis says evenly. "Maybe Bill Parcells can be like that, but I think the way NFL coaching is moving is much more to be that 'we're all in this together.' I don't know that the lack of relationship between those famous coaches and their players is a good thing these days. Many of our players here came from single-parent households, or zero-parent households. So they're looking to be led."

What other lessons does Lewis see from sports that apply to life beyond the field? "Well, I think that for young people, dealing with adversity is something you learn as an athlete, no matter what sport you play. You're not always going to win, and when you don't, you've got to take something from it and come back stronger. People also often think there's some kind of magical shortcut to success. But, of course, there is no substitute for hard work, commitment, and repetition. Another lesson is to venture out and not be afraid to fail, while learning how to compete in whatever it is that they are doing."

Among professional sports leagues, the NFL does a particularly good job of supporting local communities by raising money and having players spend time on community service. Beyond what sports can do for you at an individual level, Lewis feels strongly that sports can play a role in addressing some of society's important issues, such as tolerance of and respect for different people. "As a team, we have so many different kinds of people," Lewis says. "The diversity is key. We have white, black, and Hispanic players and people from all different backgrounds and regions. The thing a team does best, I believe, is to bring everyone together, unified around and united in achieving a singular goal. For young people, that's a great lesson, to learn to focus on the task at hand while developing essential relationships with and being mutually dependent on others. You also learn on a team that even if those other people are from a different place, are a different color, or have a different background, they are usually just like you."

THE INGREDIENT THAT BOARDS MOST LOOK FOR IN A NEW LEADER

If benevolent leadership is the way to operate once you are in the coveted management role, how do you best position yourself to actually become selected for that role in the first place? A recent experience will illustrate what is most important.

As a part of an important CEO search, I spent 2 days with the board of a major global company interviewing candidates. The directors were seated around the boardroom table, and the chairman gave a warm welcome to each candidate and set the stage for the 90-minute discussion. In a process repeated eight times during the course of the 2 days, he launched into the interview by posing the following question: "How would you assess the state of our industry and the company's position within it?" The discussion flowed from there, with every director asking different questions to probe the key areas as they saw fit.

It was a remarkably clarifying experience sitting through all of the interviews and seeing through the eyes of the directors how different candidates came across, what resonated, and what did not. It was equally noteworthy observing the dynamics of the board in its various modes of evaluation, probing, selling, and decision making. What became clearer than ever was what boards really look for when they assess CEO candidates.

In order to get to the table as a serious candidate for an important position, of course, you have to have a sufficient amount of relevant experience and a demonstrated track record of success. However, in the majority of cases, it is what actually goes on inside the boardroom during the live conversations that determines the candidate around whom the board coalesces.

The attributes that separate the best candidates from the rest are:

▶ **Intellectual prowess.** There is no underestimating the importance of sheer brain power in allowing a leader to assess a situation and develop a coherent plan of attack.

▶ **A well-founded point of view.** Boards are looking for someone to firmly stake out a position that makes sense. They are not interested in someone who is looking to them for ideas and direction about what should be done.

▶ **Superior communications skills.** Without the ability to unlock that brain power and articulate that point of view in a clear and compelling way, they might as well not exist.

▶ **Values.** There must be a strong match between what the individual stands for and what the directors and the company stand for.

▶ **Executive presence.** This is that intangible ability to inspire confidence in a group setting.

Beyond these qualities, however, there is something even more important, a capability that underlies these essential attributes and that ties them all together: the ability to think clearly. Clarity of thought is the business equivalent of mental toughness in competition. That is, the ability to think through problems proactively using your mind rather than reactively being led by your emotions. It is performing an accurate assessment of a situation and focusing your decisions around those things that are under your control rather than obsessing over exogenous factors. It is planning for contingencies and updating your action plans to take account of new information. It is about making tough personnel calls, even if it means making some people unhappy by doing so.

Mental toughness and clear thinking are so important because when boards are looking to put their trust, fiduciary responsibilities, and reputations behind a new leader, it is largely a game of confidence. Once they have selected a new CEO, the directors will leave the room and go back to their own day-to-day pressure-packed lives until the next board meeting. They will be passing the baton of accountability to the new leader to guide the company forward in a way that they can feel secure about. The board is therefore looking for someone who both understands the situation in a deep way and can develop a compelling plan of action to lead the company through the maze of issues and opportunities so as to optimize short-term and long-term results.

During those 2 days in that boardroom, the divergence among candidates along this final dimension was astonishing. The most successful were those who could: (1) explain the key competitive dynamics in the industry, i.e., what was driving change, who was winning, and who was losing and why; (2) clearly describe what the company should do to thrive, i.e., what the top priorities should be, what strategies should be pursued, and what acquisitions considered; and (3) present a sound and specific organizational "architecture" that would enable the company to move forward in a decisive and effective way, i.e., how the company should be organized, what positions should report directly to the CEO, which functions should be centralized and which pushed into the business units, and how to align incentive systems to reward the desired behaviors.

The least successful candidates were, in stark contrast, muddled in their thinking, generic in their diagnoses, unclear about the company's priorities, rambling about what strategies to pursue, and generally all over the place as to how they would organize the company going forward.

The technical term for the quality of mental toughness displayed by the strongest candidates is "executive intelligence," a concept coined by Dr. Justin Menkes in his best-selling book by the same name. Menkes, a PhD who trained under Peter Drucker, is a managing director of the Executive Intelligence Group, a leading provider of executive assessment services to global corporations.[1] Based on a decade of research on intelligence tests and management performance, Dr. Menkes found that the distinguishing characteristic of the best business leaders in the world is a set of aptitudes and cognitive skills that are at the heart of business acumen. This takes the form of an executive who asks penetrating questions, maintains a rigor in his or her thinking, and skillfully works out the best answers to tough problems by identifying and using the information that has value for that purpose (and resisting irrelevant or unreliable considerations, however tempting they may be). Just as world-class athletes have extraordinary coordination, endurance, agility, and play-making abilities (and/or other attributes depending on the sport) and the best mathematicians share an exceptional facility for computation and deductive reasoning, the best business leaders share the mental toughness and intellectual skills that enable them to create solutions tailored to suit each situation that arises.

What about inspiration and charisma as dimensions of leadership, you may ask? Inspiration, indeed, is a critical attribute of leadership. And benevolent leadership is a fail-safe way to inspire people. Charisma, by contrast, is much more hit or miss. It is, of course, that personal attractiveness that enables someone to influence others. Many successful leaders in business and public life inspire others through charisma. In popular usage—especially around the time of US presidential elections—charisma is typically bandied about as a flattering adjective. And there is little doubt in my mind that Emmitt Smith's magnetic charisma

---

[1] Executive Intelligence Group is affiliated with this author's firm, Spencer Stuart.

buttressed his newly developed ballroom dancing skills to help him capture the *Dancing with the Stars* crown in 2006. Charisma, however, has also enabled others to lead companies, even entire populations, in disastrous directions. Absent a moral anchor, charisma enables certain individuals to persuade even well-intentioned people into trouble. So charisma is not the most trustworthy quality for creating inspiration. For more on charisma and its distant but unfailingly positive etymological cousin, dynamism, see the Appendix.

The point to stress is that executive intelligence, implemented through benevolent leadership, can be accomplished just as readily by the business leader who has a deficit of charisma as by an executive who oozes charisma.

HOW TO GET OFF TO A STRONG START

A tactical dimension of performing strongly as a leader is how to take advantage of the unique opportunity that comes along when you start a new position—either as a brand-new employee starting your career or, at the other extreme, when you take the CEO reins from a predecessor.

As you launch or start a new phase of your career, it is worth reminding yourself of the old maxim that first impressions are lasting impressions. A strong start creates positive momentum—a wind at your back—which will help you perform all the more substantive actions that compose great leadership. Having a rocky start in a new role is not a mortal blow. However, it is at best an opportunity forsaken. To get you off on the right foot, or accelerate your progress along The Dynamic Path, here are six guidelines to follow:

▶ **Maintain a positive attitude.** Attitude is the single most important thing that you carry into the early days of your job. It's also something over which you have nearly complete control. Be the kind of person who creates energy rather than saps it from other people. Be upbeat and optimistic. Listen much more than you speak. Ask good questions. Don't be a know-it-all. Be proactive.

▶ **Work hard.** As explained throughout this book, there is no escaping the fact that hard work on a consistent basis is an essential requirement for success—at all levels. So as you start your career, get into the office early. Stay late. But don't work hard just to create face time. Do so to get more high-quality work done. You can still work hard and find time to keep your personal life, family obligations, and physical self in shape. In fact, if you *don't* find or make time for all these things, you will find yourself unable to perform at peak levels for a sustainable period of time. In other words, *unless* you have a contented family life and stay in shape, you are unlikely to truly succeed. Take advantage of the time shifting that e-mail and communications technology make possible in today's workplace to figure out how to work hard in a way that works for you.

▶ **Deliver on your commitments.** Become known as someone who can be counted on to successfully complete whatever task is requested on time and with high quality. You should expect that your first job will be narrowly defined, so some of your early assignments might seem menial. They aren't. Delivering on your commitments builds trust and confidence. You'll be surprised how quickly larger and more significant assignments flow your way when you develop this reputation.

▶ **Do completed staff work.** Completed staff work is a concept that I learned as an associate at McKinsey & Company. This means going beyond the rote to understand why something is asked for and how it'll be used when it's completed. If a client-service executive asks you for an analysis of a target account, for example, completed staff work will be a finished product that can be proudly passed along to your boss's boss or to the client itself. Set this as the standard for all of your work.

▶ **Focus on the success of others.** Embrace the benevolent leadership philosophy from day one of your career and make it a habit. It's a guaranteed success strategy that if you make others around you successful, then you'll be successful as a natural consequence. Even as a new employee, this will make the most talented people in the organization want you to work with them. You will be in demand for the most important projects by the most senior people, and you will build a network of supporters across the organization who are pulling for your success. But how, you may ask, can I help others be successful if I'm brand-new in the job myself? Look for ways to be helpful. Be proactive. Be willing to take on extra or unpopular work. Keep focused on the goals of your boss, your team, and your company ahead of your own goals.

▶ **Understand your boss's motivations.** Most managers in business will say that their goals are to grow revenues, control costs, develop a winning strategy, make sound investments, and manage people effectively. While these ambitions are usually genuine, they generally represent only a portion of how bosses really think and act. They have additional underlying motivations, which, while less idealistic, are no less real. According to David D'Alessandro, former CEO of insurance giant John Hancock Financial Services and author of the best-selling book *Career Warfare*, "What bosses want more than anything else is loyalty, good advice, and to have 'their personal brands polished.'" Bosses don't want yes-men or -women who offer insincere flattery, or downers who play devil's advocate or who make themselves look good at the boss's expense. Most people instinctively separate the individuals they manage into three distinct categories: the sycophants, the contrarians, and the small percentage of their employees who are the balanced players. You definitely want to be seen as one in the third group. You might be surprised at how influential you can be, regardless of your hierarchical level, by becoming known as a source of good ideas, thoughtful perspectives, support, and creative solutions.

TAKING OVER FROM A POWERFUL LEADER

Congratulations. You've succeeded. You now find yourself in the situation of assuming responsibility for an entire organization. It is now time to put the principles of benevolent leadership into high gear. However, if you are tapped to succeed a powerful, and in many cases charismatic, leader, you will have additional challenges to address. This was the case for Bob Iger in taking over from Michael Eisner at The Walt Disney Company, Mark Hurd in succeeding Carly Fiorina at Hewlett-Packard Company, and Jeff Immelt in following Jack Welch at General Electric Company. Each had to figure out how to lead in a way that was entirely their own, but one that worked for the company. Based on the many hundreds of CEO searches led by Spencer Stuart and our study of 100 of the best and worst CEO successions,[2] here are five additional guidelines for starting a new leadership position, especially when taking over from a powerful and charismatic chief executive:

▶ **Be your own person.** Don't try to be someone you're not. As Jeff Immelt said shortly after becoming GE's CEO, "I'd never try to 'out-Jack' Jack." Let your predecessor's style go out with your predecessor. Also, regardless of whether you are coming in from the outside or have spent your entire career at the company, make

---

[2] The study was done for the book *You're in Charge, Now What?*, co-authored by my partner, Thomas J. Neff, and myself, and published in January 2005.

sure to introduce (or reintroduce) yourself to the organization and answer the questions on people's minds: "Who am I? Why am I here? What do I believe/what are my values? What do I hope to accomplish?"

▶ **It's not about you.** It's about the company and the people who work there, the customers you serve, and the investors who are looking for an attractive return. Give credit to others for successes and use "we" not "I"—except when shouldering blame. This is just another way to exercise the benevolent leadership approach that inspires people.

▶ **Establish three powerful themes.** Develop *three* straightforward themes and use them consistently and relentlessly in order to bring focus and high performance to the organization. The three themes (two come across as incomplete and people won't remember four) need to be specific enough to be meaningful, yet general enough to serve as organizing principles for all of the company's businesses and functions. Simplicity and clarity are almost always more important than comprehensiveness and precision.

▶ **Let your actions do your talking.** When Bob Iger became CEO, he said that Disney was going to focus on creating great content and storytelling, apply technology in the creation and distribution of the company's businesses, and work in a more entrepreneurial, less bureaucratic way. He quickly brought his themes to life through the decisions and transactions to rebuild the relationship with and acquire Pixar and do the first deal to sell television downloads on Apple's Video iPod, among many other things.

▶ **Never "diss" your predecessor.** In all but the most horrible situations, never speak ill of your predecessor. Especially if he or she was a charismatic leader (for better or worse); there will still be people within the organization who are nostalgic for the former CEO.

Preserving a sense of continuity with the past and demonstrating genuine respect for the prior regime will establish you as a class act and seasoned leader.

If you do find yourself taking over from a great leader, remember that your predecessor was by definition no longer an individual champion, even if it may have appeared that way to the outside world. Attempting to practice charismatic leadership through individual achievement writ large, as opposed to benevolent leadership for collective results, is the best way to ignore all of the advice in these guidelines.

◆

Howard Schultz's
Perfect Brew

I first met Starbucks founder and chairman Howard Schultz at his home in the summer of 1998 and will never forget the experience, and not just for the coffee. We were sitting on his deck sipping from mugs emblazoned with the company's famous siren symbol, discussing how his leadership philosophy was shaped by difficult boyhood family circumstances. Howard's father, a blue-collar worker, was injured on the job while working for a company with no health insurance or any other means of support. He lost his job and the family was forced to move to low-income public housing, "the projects," in Brooklyn. Howard watched his father's self-esteem and health wither. He vowed that if he was ever in a position of responsibility one day in the future, he would never let happen to others what happened to his father.

In a story befitting Horatio Alger, Howard got his break from sports. A talented athlete, he was quarterback of the Canarsie High School football team. One day in the fall of his senior year, a scout from Northern Michigan University came to watch a game. Only he wasn't there to scout Howard, he was there to look at the quarterback on the other team. His head was turned by Schultz's performance and, after throwing for multiple touchdowns and leading his team on the field with grace and discipline, it was Howard who got the football scholarship. Schultz thrived at NMU and, after graduation, got a job with Xerox, where he became a star performer.

Several years later, following his passion and taking a risk, Schultz went to work for the single Starbucks Coffee, Tea, and Spices store in Seattle's Pike Place Market. On vacation in Italy, he took note of the coffee bars that existed on practically every block. He learned that they not only served excellent espresso, they also served as public meeting places and cultural glue. Inspired by the Italian café culture and sensing the commercial opportunity in the United States—there were 200,000 coffee bars in Italy alone—Howard proposed expanding the store's business from only selling coffees and teas to establishing coffee bars. When his bosses did not agree, he left to found a small chain of espresso bars in Seattle; several years later, he came back and acquired the original Starbuck's shop, paying $3.8 million for the store, the name, and the logo.[3]

From the start, Howard wanted to build a company with soul, high on trust and motivation. Remembering his father's struggles, he was committed to providing full medical benefits and stock options for *all* employees. He genuinely believed—and still believes—that the best way to deliver the greatest customer experience is to deliver the best employee experience. Howard's leadership philosophy has turned out to be a winning financial strategy as well. The benefits and stock-options program has paid for itself in dramatically reduced turnover and higher morale. Today, Starbucks has nearly 14,000 stores in 37 countries and has a market capitalization of $22 billion. The company is consistently ranked as one of the best places to work and has become America's second-most-admired company (behind GE). Howard is the architect of what

[3] For Starbucks trivia fans, the company is named for the first mate of Herman Melville's *Moby-Dick*. Howard made one major change to the original logo. He took the mermaid's hair and moved it from behind her back to in front of her chest, thereby making it more appropriate for customers of all ages!

the Starbucks brand represents, serves as an international ambassador for the company, and imbues the organization with its special culture. He continues to be deeply passionate about what he does—building a lifestyle brand that serves tens of millions of customers, developing great people, drinking delicious coffee, and having a positive impact on the world.

MORE SERIOUS THAN LIFE AND DEATH

"QUESTION: IS WINNING THE ALL BLACKS-WALES INTERNATIONAL TEST MATCH THE DIFFERENCE BETWEEN LIFE AND DEATH?
"ANSWER: NO, IT IS A LOT MORE SERIOUS THAN THAT."
—SEAN FITZPATRICK
Captain, New Zealand All Blacks Rugby, 1992–1997

For more than 100 years, the New Zealand All Blacks have been the world's foremost team in the sport of rugby, a game of brute force, speed, and finesse. No other sports team in the world has achieved a 72 percent winning percentage over the course of a century. It is an amazing fact that a tiny nation of four million (where there are more sheep than people) can produce the greatest team in the history of any sport. Aside from tiny New Zealand, the best rugby countries in the world are Australia, France, Ireland, England, Scotland, Wales, Italy, Canada, Argentina, and South Africa. The game is also rapidly gaining popularity in Japan and the United States.

Sean Fitzpatrick, captain of the All Blacks from 1992 until his retirement in 1997, is considered to be the greatest All Blacks captain of all time. With his durability, competitiveness, and dynamic playmaking in the position of hooker, he was one of the best players in the history of the sport. However, beyond his dominance on the field, it was and continues to be his leadership off the field that makes him widely regarded as the greatest All Blacks leader of all time. Through his clear goal setting, respect for his predecessors, leadership by example, management of cultural change, and decisive yet benevolent leadership, he embodied the proud spirit of All Blacks rugby and is a stellar role model for all who aspire to lead.

Fitzpatrick's position, the hooker, is the player in the middle of the scrum who has to withstand about 600 pounds of opposing players on top of him and 2,000 pounds of force pushing against his neck. In this demanding position, he played a record 92 test matches [international competitions] for the All Blacks between 1986 and 1997, 51 of which were as captain, also a record.

Fitzpatrick remained remarkably healthy on the field for many years, but in 1997 an injured knee forced him to retire from active play. After stepping down as a player, he remained involved in the game, adding to his iconic status by working as an ambassador for the game, managing two New Zealand national teams, and in 2004 becoming a television commentator in Britain.

"I love rugby because it's very much a team game," Fitzpatrick says, evidencing the foundational philosophy of benevolent leadership. "I know that sounds sort of trite, but I love the ethos that goes with the team game. On the team, we're all equal, all contributing to the singular goal of winning. You may have six different stars on a team, but at the end of the day, we're all the same. If the team loses, even if you score five tries (touchdownlike scores), you're devastated. I just love the fact that you look after your mates. It's very important to make sure that you're the best you can be, not only for yourself, but for the sake of your mates."

Rugby is different from other sports. There is a long tradition of ferocity on the field juxtaposed with camaraderie off the field. Teams go from archenemies, stoked by battlefield emotions, to drinking buddies in the clubhouse right after the game. "It's a Jekyll and Hyde phenomenon," Fitzpatrick says. "I'm a Gemini, so I'm suited for it. But yes, it's a nice thing to do after games. It's one of those traditions passed down from generation to generation. We've long been told, when the game's over, you go and shout your opposite a beer. I was a different man on the field, where I was hugely competitive, and off the field, where I'm pretty nice."

Great leaders draw inspiration from tradition and putting the team's efforts in a historical context at the moment of truth. Nowhere is this more evident than with the All Blacks' pregame ritual, the *haka*. Fitzpatrick explains the *haka* and its significance: "It was a traditional war dance used by the Māori tribes in New Zealand when they went into battle. They also performed it when they came back from war to celebrate victory. Traditionally when the warriors left their communities, they would perform a *haka* to say to their enemy, 'We are going out to war, we are going to fight you, we are going to rip your head off and slit your throat.'

"A minute before we play a game, we do the *haka*. On the night before game day, we talk about our game plan and then we practice the *haka*. When we do it at the game, it serves as a trigger. Everyone knows exactly what our goals are, what we're going to do right from the kickoff, and what each one of us is going to deliver. It brings the team around so that all of our actions reinforce one another. Once a year, we arrange for a Māori chief to come in and talk to the team about the *haka* and demonstrate the correct way to stand, to gesture, and to chant. All the moves are about summoning and conveying strength."

When I met Fitzpatrick in London for the first time, at the moment in our conversation when he finished describing the *haka*, he jumped up from his chair and performed the ritual with intense chanting and gesturing. "What was that fearsome motion at the end?" I asked.

"When we jump in the air, the motion is grabbing your hair and then, ugh! breaking your neck. And I finish by grabbing a knife and slitting your throat! The *haka* is done with huge passion. It's fantastic," Fitzpatrick concludes with a satiated smile.

ONCE AN ALL BLACK, ALWAYS AN ALL BLACK

As captain, Fitzpatrick also invoked the expectations of the nation to inspire the team. "It's not a money thing," he says. "It's about the people that have come before us. We speak a lot about the players of old. We have them come and talk to us about their times and why they were successful. The first time I played on the team, the veterans came in and talked about what it means to be an All Black. We were so moved by what they were saying that we cried. If you look at the best players in New Zealand, the reason they stay in the country is because they want to play for the All Blacks. In Europe, they could earn three times what they make down there. And once they become an All Black, they are expected to win. There are four million 'shareholders' in New Zealand, and every single one of them expects you to work harder than anyone and to defeat all comers. So you go out there, and you do everything you can to make sure you do that.

"That's where the 'English mentality' differs from the All Black," Fitzpatrick adds. What's the English mentality? "'Oh, jolly good, we tried our hardest, but the best team won.' For us, though, winning and heart are everything. That's what gives us the edge."

Although most students of rugby assume that the All Blacks have always had their winning culture, it was not at all the case when Fitzpatrick became captain in 1992. Like a new chief executive appointed by the board to revitalize a once-winning company, Fitzpatrick took over a franchise that had lost its way. From 1986, when he got to the All Blacks, through 1991, the team was as successful as ever. But in 1991, that all changed. They lost the World Cup and other important test matches and developed a crisis of confidence. The team did a nearly total housecleaning. Of the 30 players who went to the World Cup in 1991, only six remained the following year.

When Fitzpatrick became captain, the team was almost starting from scratch. He determined that fundamental cultural change was needed on the team. "The team had developed these rules," Fitzpatrick says, "such as 'The young guys don't mingle.' They weren't supposed to talk to the older guys unless spoken to. And they were not to ask questions. I realized that the culture was blocking change and knew that was holding us all back. We were all one team here."

So Fitzpatrick led a change in how the team operated. "I started speaking to the older players the same way I spoke to the younger players, with no more and no less respect. I was very inclusive of the younger guys and encouraged them to put their hands up during team meetings. Before that time, they never dared ask a question. I put an enormous emphasis on creating an open environment, one where you could question authority. It took a lot of courage for players to start asking direct questions like 'Why do we do it this way?' It also took courage for players to admit their mistakes. When watching game videos at the beginning of the new team, we had to reduce the barriers to honest evaluation by writing observations about ourselves down on pieces of paper. After a while, we were able to talk about it all amongst ourselves instead of writing it down."

As the culture of the team improved, it carried over into the quality of the team's play on the field. Great leadership is also about results, and behind Fitzpatrick, the All Blacks soon got back to their winning ways.

When it comes to being a leader, Fitzpatrick believes that the most important thing is earning the respect of the players. "The first thing I worked on," he says, "was demonstrating that I deserved to have the job. The easiest way to do that was to train harder than anyone else and play the best rugby. I'm a big believer that respect is probably the number-one ingredient in effective leadership. If someone doesn't respect you, you're never going to get anything out of them. Ever. You can't ask someone to do something that you wouldn't do yourself. I say to people who want to lead, 'You don't need to be liked, but you need to be respected.' I'm sure the players that played under me probably didn't like me. But they respected me. I'm happier there."

These same words could just as easily be said by the best leaders in business. If you want to be a great leader, make Fitzpatrick's words, beliefs, and actions your own.

CHAPTER 8

Dynamic Moment III

Finding a Calling

Each of us, in our own individuality, has the opportunity to find a calling, the first step in moving beyond the here and now toward establishing an enduring legacy. A framework for this is provided each year in the form of New Year's resolutions, a well-worn ritual followed (for a few days at least) by more than 100 million Americans. In some traditions, the opportunity comes each weekend on a Saturday or Sunday morning. In other traditions, it comes five times a day when facing Mecca, and in others it presents itself annually each autumn on the Day of Atonement, Yom Kippur.

Before finding a calling to dedicate an important part of your life to, it is helpful to become regrounded in the eternal values on which moral and spiritual leadership are based. A thought process borrowed from Judaism that I have found useful in doing just this is to specifically reflect on the year gone by and wrestle with how to make substantive improvements for the year ahead, including coming closer to finding a calling.

Each of us has abilities endowed by nature and by the circumstances of our lives. Whether I have done better or worse with my own capacities than others have with theirs, I cannot and need not judge. But I can and should contemplate the degree to which I:

▶ *Have worked as conscientiously and energetically as possible.*

▶ *Have been focused on the well-being of those individuals who depend on me.*

▶ *Have maintained discipline to resist the myriad temptations that are omnipresent in life today.*

▶ *Have prioritized my attention, concentration, and efforts on the truly important versus merely urgent things in a world with an excess of stimuli.*

▶ *Have moved closer toward realizing my individualized potential.*

▶ *Have taken advantage of the opportunities afforded by my professional position to make my core beliefs a reality.*

▶ *Have strived not for perfection but for being the very best I can be.*

In other words, what is most important to you and what do you stand for? How do all of your day-to-day decisions and actions roll up into something greater than yourself? Unless you are a saint, however, these questions are somewhat rhetorical and have to be balanced within the reality of your life, how you make a living, and what family and community responsibilities you shoulder.

Let's take a look at how one prominent leader worked to strike the right balance for himself and, in so doing, identified the legacy he wished to leave.

"JUST CALL ME COLIN"

In April 2005, I was sitting in a modest office on the top floor of a red brick office building in Alexandria, Virginia. On the wall behind the round conference table were several plaques and photographs of assorted world leaders. "Sorry to be a little unfamiliar with the right conventions," I said to the imposing person sitting across from me, "but what is the appropriate way to address you? General Powell? Or Secretary Powell?"

Through a warm smile and in a melodious voice, he replied, "How about just Colin?"

What in the world was *I* doing meeting with the former secretary of state of the United States? Actually, I was there for a one-on-one career strategy working session for his life after the Bush Administration.

One morning in January 2005, through an introduction from Jackie Arends, one of my Spencer Stuart partners, who before joining our firm had worked at the White House, I put a call into Secretary Powell's office. As it happened, my call, which was to explore his potential interest in moving into the private sector, was rather well timed. Just 2 hours later, he announced his decision to step down as secretary of state.

Anyone who had been following the news knew that shortly after the 2005 inauguration of President Bush for his second term, Secretary Powell would be leaving the administration. I figured that whenever that was to be, he might want to consider his options in the widest possible terms. I had been working on an executive search assignment to recruit a chairman for a giant media corporation, and I thought that Secretary Powell might be an inspired choice. A few hours later, I got a call back from his chief of staff, who said, "First of all, the secretary extends his appreciation to you for being the very first person to approach him with an offer on the day of his announcement. However, he will not be able to consider this until Secretary Condoleezza Rice's confirmation. At that point, we will have him call you." True to his word, about a month later, my assistant e-mailed me with the message: "You received a call from Colin Powell—personally. Please call him ASAP." Try as I might, I just could not resist showing the e-mail on my Treo to the colleague sitting next to me in the meeting.

Colin Powell is one of the most revered and admired individuals in America and one of the most respected statesmen in US history. A fervent promoter of democratic values, he was unanimously confirmed by the US Senate and became the 65th secretary of state in January 2001. Previously, General Powell served as a key aide to the secretary of defense and as national security advisor to President Reagan. He also served 35 years in the US Army, rising to the rank of four-star general. During his tenure as chairman of the Joint Chiefs of Staff, he oversaw 28 crises, including Operation Desert Storm in the 1991 Persian Gulf War. Powell is the recipient of numerous US military awards, two Presidential Medals of Freedom, and the Congressional Gold Medal. He has also received a French *Légion d'honneur* and an honorary knighthood bestowed by Queen Elizabeth II of Great Britain.

On my phone call, he greeted me in a warm voice, saying that he had gone to the bookstore the day before and bought our just-released book, *You're in Charge, Now What?*. "How did that come to *your* attention?" I asked in mild disbelief.

"I read the review in yesterday's *Wall Street Journal*," he said. "What you wrote about listening and learning, not coming in with all the answers, and also not becoming trapped in analysis paralysis, is entirely consistent with my own experience. When I came into State, I found one of the most dysfunctional organizations known to man. They had white papers for the white papers. I told them, 'Enough studying things to death to get the perfect answer, let's do something!'"

With that nice lead-in, I felt even more comfortable pitching Secretary Powell on the merits of taking all of his experience communicating through the media, setting strategy, making people decisions, and determining priorities and applying all of these skills in the private sector. We had an engaging discussion about some of the many things he could do and how the particular opportunity that had led me to call him might fit in. Toward the end of this call, I had the idea to suggest that rather than making this or any decision in isolation, I should come in and see him in Washington, D.C., to help him think through the various opportunities that would be possible for him. He welcomed this idea.

With that plan in place, I immediately went out and purchased Powell's bestseller, *My American Journey*. As I read it, I looked for clues about his leadership and any hot buttons that might allow me to present my recommendations in the most effective way possible. My favorite passage from the book is a great summation of Powell's leadership philosophy:

> *"For years, I have told young officers that most of what I know about military life I learned in my first 8 weeks at Fort Benning [Georgia, basic infantry training]. I can sum those lessons in a few maxims:*
>
> ▶ *"Take charge of this post and all government property in view"—the Army's first general order.*
>
> ▶ *The mission is primary, followed by taking care of your soldiers.*
>
> ▶ *Don't stand there. Do something!*
>
> ▶ *Lead by example.*
>
> ▶ *"No excuse, sir."*
>
> ▶ *Officers always eat last.*
>
> ▶ *Never forget, you're an American infantryman, the best.*
>
> ▶ *And never be without a watch, a pencil, and a notepad.*

COMPENSATION, LIFESTYLE, AND IMPACT

What do you do next after you've been secretary of state and chairman of the Joint Chiefs of Staff and you are one of the most visible and respected citizens of the world? To help answer this vexing question, I prepared a brief presentation introducing the "Career Triangle," a framework for how the secretary might think about his seemingly unlimited opportunities. This was based on the fundamental forces that govern all careers, not just those at the pinnacle of influence and recognition. A career decision at any moment in time is essentially a search to optimize three generally competing forces: the impact and inherent qualities of the role itself, lifestyle issues, and compensation/financial considerations. I explained to him that while it would be relatively easy to achieve his goals on one or even two of these dimensions, the art in career decisions is to find the right balance among all three.

For example, for Colin—as I now had permission to call him—after a long and distinguished career in public service, he certainly had the ability to maximize the financial opportunities available to him—and it would be completely understandable to do so. Like presidents, prime ministers, and cabinet secretaries before him, he could earn millions by joining one of the major private equity firms that trade on stature, influence, and access. He could also be handsomely rewarded by agreeing to lend his credibility and door-opening capabilities to one of the giant global financial institutions as a vice chairman or member of their advisory board. Alternatively, he could earn many hundreds of thousands of dollars by becoming a professional corporate director, accepting invitations from four or five of the countless major corporations who would be eager to have him bring his judgment, global perspective, and stature to their board. He could create his own lobbying firm, generating large sums by using his influence to shape legislation for clients who would be only too happy to pay up. Or, he could hit the speaking circuit, picking up about $150,000 per engagement by speaking to groups of people and organizations hungry for his leadership lessons, and of course a photo op.

But after an exhausting work and travel schedule over many years that required him to be away from his beloved wife, Alma, and family, he would in all likelihood want to consider the lifestyle dimension of anything he chose to do next. He would presumably want to have more control over his work and travel schedule as well as where he lived, and to have the ability to be where he wanted to be when he wanted to be there. Indeed, he confirmed that lifestyle was an important consideration in terms of hours, predictability, and control over his schedule. "I promised Alma," he said, "that I wouldn't work so hard and that I would be more available at home." It would be relatively easy to maximize the lifestyle dimension. How? He could work from home writing a new book. He could take on a board role in one or several local Washington, D.C., organizations. He could take on a limited speaking schedule with bookings committed to far in advance.

Even if he used this opportunity to catch up on time with his family and/or to earn the kind of income that he went without over 3 decades, you don't have a career like that of Colin Powell without having a deep commitment to making an impact on the world. Any new role would surely also have to have a deeper mission to it.

We ran half a dozen ideas through this filter—as shown on the illustrations below and on the following page. He decided to take a pass, unfortunately, on the media chairmanship.

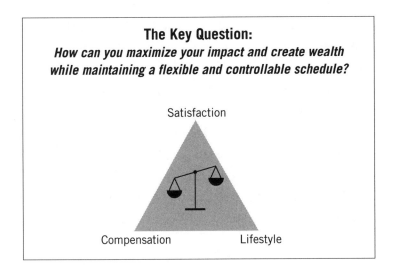

The Key Question:
How can you maximize your impact and create wealth while maintaining a flexible and controllable schedule?

Satisfaction

Compensation   Lifestyle

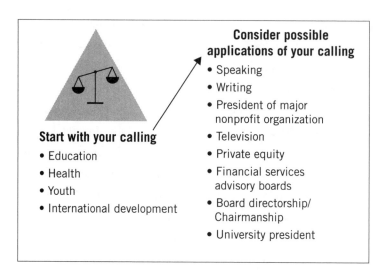

My impressions of Colin were that he is a completely genuine person who has an inner strength based on values, a natural optimism and faith in the inherent goodness of people, and a belief that sometimes giving the tough medicine is in fact the most compassionate course, balanced by a worldly sophistication rooted in a nuanced understanding of geopolitical history.

So what did Secretary Powell finally decide to do? He chose a "portfolio" of activities that, taken together, meet all three objectives, financial, lifestyle, and impact. He accepted speaking engagements around the world—including one by Spencer Stuart to address our worldwide partnership. He became affiliated with two prominent private investment firms, one of which has a long-running, top-performing track record of returns and the other of which is still in the early stages. However, both firms have deep financial resources and leaders dedicated to using them to not only generate superior financial returns for their investors, but also to make as much positive change in the world as possible.

Powell joined Kleiner Perkins Caufield & Byers, the prominent Silicon Valley venture capital firm, as a strategic limited partner. Led by John Doerr, Kleiner Perkins has been instrumental in the formation of more than 475 companies since its founding in 1972, including such transformers as Google, Amazon.com, Sun Microsystems, and Genentech. Doerr himself is not only prominent from an investment perspective—Cisco Systems CEO John Chambers calls Doerr "the single best venture capitalist in the world"—but he is also at the forefront of attacking urgent world priorities. He is committed to supporting entrepreneurs working to prevent pandemic avian flu and the spread of other global infectious diseases and is also passionately interested in improving public education, the environment, global poverty, and health. These issues resonate with Colin.

Powell also joined with AOL founder Steve Case in his firm, Revolution LLC, founded in April 2005 and based in Washington, D.C. Revolution is a private holding company that Case has personally funded with $500 million to invest in health care, wellness, and resorts—three sectors in which he sees significant sustained growth. Powell, who got to know Case while serving on the board of America Online when it was an independent public company, was particularly attracted to Case's vision for using technology and the Internet to usher in a consumer-led overhaul of the nation's out-of-control health care system.

Powell's perch at Kleiner Perkins and Revolution allows him to continue his decade of work on one of the causes that he views as a calling, improving the lives of America's youth. In 1997, he was the founding chairman of America's Promise—The Alliance for Youth. This organization grew out of a meeting in Philadelphia called the Presidents' Summit for America's Future, at which Presidents Clinton, Bush (41), Carter, and Ford, along with Nancy Reagan representing President Reagan, developed a manifesto to make children and youth a national priority in the United States.

The summit—also attended by nearly 30 governors, 100 mayors, 145 community delegations, and prominent business leaders—was sponsored by the Points of Light Foundation, the Corporation for National and Community Service, and the United Way. It sought to attack the urgent problems of large segments of the youth population, such as:

▶ Nearly two-thirds of African American children and almost one in four white children live in a household with only one parent.

▶ Two million American children have a parent in jail.

▶ 740,000 children were victims of violent crimes in their schools in 2003.

▶ 34 percent of African American children live in poverty.

▶ In 2004, approximately one in five 10th graders reported using illegal drugs within the past 30 days.

▶ Approximately one in 11 high school students reported attempting suicide in 2003.

▶ Approximately 5,000 children committed suicide in 2001.

▶ Approximately 30 percent of US students do not finish high school.

▶ 70 percent of eighth graders score below proficiency levels in math, and 69 percent score below proficiency in English.

Since its establishment, the America's Promise alliance has grown into a dynamic network of organizations comprising corporations, nonprofits, higher education groups, religious organizations, associations, federal agencies, and community groups. From the time of the organization's formation, Powell was hands-on as chairman, and he proudly cites its impact:

▶ 2 million more young people now have mentors.

▶ 3 million more children now have safe places where they can routinely go.

▶ 4 million more children now have health insurance.

▶ 4 million more young people have now received introductions to the working world through job shadowing.

▶ 1.2 million young people are now volunteering more than 100 hours every year.

Today, building on the Powell leadership efforts, Alma Powell has taken over as chairperson of the America's Promise alliance.

Overall, I would say that Colin Powell has gotten his next career phase off to a very good start.

THE TIME IS NOW

You don't have to wait until you retire from your primary career to "step back" and think about when and how to start building a legacy. Colin Powell didn't wait until he left his post as secretary of state to take action on the causes that are most important to him. Billie Jean King didn't start working to achieve equality for women only after completing her championship tennis career, and Tiger was still relatively early in his life as a pro when he launched the Tiger Woods Foundation. In fact, the three major stages of The Dynamic Path—champion, leader, and legacy—don't even necessarily have to occur sequentially. The greatest champions, for example, are those who also lead others to greatness and who also stand for something larger and more important than themselves.

You also don't have to be famous or wealthy to find a calling and build a legacy. Just take a careful look around you. Who are the people whom everyone most respects in your community and your organization? I would wager that they are not only those who are the most "successful" in the traditional sense. Where my family and I live, for example, there is one person who has catalyzed the entire town with her leadership and energy. Sally Campbell is the mom of five sons, all of whom are stellar students and superior athletes. She has personally led the organization of many town sports, hiring and managing various coaches and even leading the varsity lacrosse team on a spring training trip to Florida. Sally also led the planning and fund-raising campaign to rebuild the town's fields and has been a regular team parent, hosting team dinners and organizing the efforts of other parents. Even though she doesn't currently apply her Wharton MBA at a company, she has as important an impact on as many people as many chief executives.

70 MILLION YELLOW LIVESTRONG WRISTBANDS

Tony Hawk is not unlike many other champions and leaders whom I met over the course of researching and writing this book. Whom does he admire most among sports leaders? "Lance Armstrong," Hawk says without hesitation. "I think he's one of the best examples of discipline, hard work, and inspiration. Being such a great champion is one part of it, but his focus and determination as a cancer survivor is the other important part.

"I can see that that's the path that Lance is on," Hawk adds. "I really identify with him now, especially in that like Lance, I don't compete anymore and people think we're retired, so to speak. But I'm still skating as much as ever, doing plenty of exhibitions and shows and raising money for the foundation." With the Tony Hawk Foundation and his business interests, he says that he is working harder than when he was competing. "But it's not about the competition anymore; there's just so much important work that needs to be done."

Tony Hawk is surely not unique in his admiration of Lance Armstrong. Beyond his lucrative endorsement deals and best-selling books, just consider the story of Lance's signature yellow "Livestrong" bracelets.

Launched in May 2004, the "Livestrong" wristband, made of yellow silicone rubber, was created to allow people to visibly and financially support the Lance Armstrong Foundation and its cancer research program. Lance says that it was Nike and their ad agency Wieden+Kennedy that came up with the idea as a way to raise money for cancer research (and if it also *happened* to extend the Nike brand, so much the better). The original plan was to make five million of them and charge $1 each, with the objective of generating up to $5 million for the foundation. But the bands mushroomed into a social phenomenon and the original goal was achieved in 6 months. The first major exposure occurred in the summer of 2004, when the bands were worn by a majority of the riders in that year's Tour de France and by a wide variety of athletes at the 2004 Olympics in Athens. Soon, with personalities such as 2004 Democratic presidential candidate John Kerry and news anchor Katie Couric visibly wearing the wristbands, they became the must-have item for athletes, businesspeople, students, fathers, mothers, and world leaders. The force of the movement stemmed from the fact that the band is simple and is a symbol with which people want to be associated. Today, Lance estimates that the total is about 70 million.

"As an athlete, it's a tremendous honor," Lance says. "Something happened that I can't exactly define that really clicked with different groups of people. To me, it was an amazing thing to see the yellow wristband being worn by other athletes at the Olympic Games. You started to see athletes from all over the world, all religions, all races, and all nationalities, wearing the band.

"The most memorable moment for me was to see the band being worn by Hicham El Guerrouj, the Moroccan running star. Here's arguably the most powerful Muslim athlete in the world, who arrived in Athens with a bunch of world records, but who had never won an Olympic gold. Then he crossed the finish line first in both the 1,500- and 5,000-meter races and he was wearing the yellow band. Seeing El Guerrouj on the ground praying to Allah wearing the yellow band told me that life isn't a question of one set of values versus another; it can be something transcendent.

"My life goal now is at the end of it all to be remembered not for cycling, but for having made a huge impact on getting rid of cancer," Lance says. "Cancer is my thing. I'm Lance and I'm a cancer survivor. I've really decided to focus solely on that. It's a big-enough problem that I think it needs my full attention and energy." This was not a fanciful comment. It was deeply genuine and authentic.

Of course, the Lance Armstrong brand will be more difficult to sustain now that his big window of promotion, the Tour de France, is a thing of the past. How is he thinking about keeping the brand alive after retirement? "Traditionally, this doesn't happen," Lance says. "When athletes retire, they are replaced by the next great athlete, the next record breaker, the next name, the next personality, and they put you out to pasture. Ironically, though, for me, we're not seeing that. We just redid my Nike deal for a few more years and are closing on other major deals. Some people will tell you that retired athletes are now safer. What I need to do, however, is not so much about finding new deals, going after the brand, or keeping the brand alive. It's about finding a few key partners and totally utilizing my time to the best of my ability. That's the way I can have the largest impact."

If Lance is the sports leader Tony Hawk admires most, who does Lance admire?

Andre Agassi.

"Andre is the guy that I admire the most; it's not even close. He was around for so long and definitely worked the hardest of anyone I know. His training regimen and his work at the gym were legendary. He really rededicated himself; I can't say enough good things about him. The other reason is what he's done off the tennis court. I've been to Andre's fundraiser to support his school in Las Vegas. He is so passionate about that, and it's making a big impact. This is the real thing."

MY OWN PERSONAL CALLING

Not everyone can be a Colin Powell, Lance Armstrong, or Andre Agassi. Happily, not everyone has to be. It may sound trite, but I believe it very deeply—you just have to be the best you can be. I promise you, each of the champions, leaders, and legacy builders that I've come to know is striving to be no more and no less than the best he or she can be.

While it's relatively easy to write about how others have found a calling, it's tougher, but also more important, to decide to find a calling for yourself. I've been a big goal setter and New Year's resolution person for a long time. Today, in reflecting on what I consider my own personal calling, my thinking starts with a set of core beliefs. I then consider how to align my goals and actions with these beliefs.

I've never been one to talk about or really even maintain beliefs strong enough that I thought were worth fighting for. But over the last couple of years, as I've met and spoken to some of the most inspiring people out there, that has changed. Because of their influence (and perhaps my own maturation), my fundamental beliefs, listed here, have come into much sharper focus.

▶ While people's skills, abilities, and resources differ sharply, one person is no better or worse than another person.

▶ No one individual, group, or faith has a monopoly on truth and righteousness.

▶ There are many different forms of expressing one's beliefs; none necessarily is more valid than another. As a result, each person has the right to express his or her beliefs in the way he or she sees fit, as long as that does not harm someone else.

▶ One should learn about, respect, and celebrate others' differences, even if a part of human nature creates fear and distrust of people who look or speak differently.

▶ People generally need and want similar things: food, shelter, love, communication, a sense of belonging to a community, and an opportunity to try to become the best that they can be.

▶ Just about everyone loves their families and children infinitely. If forced, I would give my life up for any member of my nuclear family.

▶ Obviously, human beings have been endowed with the capability, and in some cases the desire, to wage battle and war. But the inherent impulses that create these feelings—the adrenaline rush, sense of honor, power, recognition, prestige, lust, desire for wealth—can also be channeled into productive and positive causes.

▶ It is essential to learn from your own mistakes and successes and those of others as well as to learn from history.

▶ Almost all important work in the present era is done in and through organizations.

▶ If I can "do it," then so too can anyone. If you focus, work hard, and are committed to learning and to working with and through others, then almost anyone can find a way to do amazing things.

The implications of these core beliefs are to:

▶ Not only tolerate, but celebrate people's differences and similarities.

▶ Never give up, never give up hope, and never stop trying to make the world a closer reflection of my core beliefs.

▶ Concentrate, channel, and leverage my efforts and resources through my primary institution—Spencer Stuart—and other affiliations, networks, and relationships to nudge the world closer to my core beliefs.

▶ Continue to strive for excellence in building clients' top leadership teams and helping individuals realize their professional aspirations and their own potential.

▶ Be a thought leader and people leader in a manner that is consistent with my core beliefs.

What are your fundamental beliefs? How well are you living them? Perhaps the thought processes and examples outlined in this chapter can help stimulate your thinking about what is truly most important to you, and that will help you find your calling and allow you to start building your legacy.

CHAPTER 9

Lessons in
Legacy Building

Track star Wilma Rudolph won three gold medals for the United States at the 1960 Olympic Games in Rome and a bronze in the 1956 Games in Melbourne. However, her achievements extended beyond the realm of sport into education. While that is legacy enough, the challenges that she overcame along her way to becoming a champion and a leader are an immortal source of inspiration to those who come after her.

On June 23, 1940, in St. Bethlehem, Tennessee, Wilma Rudolph was born the 20th of 22 children in her family (from two marriages). She was born prematurely, weighing only 4½ pounds. Rudolph spent most of her childhood in bed, suffering from double pneumonia, scarlet fever, and whooping cough. Then when she was 4, to make matters indescribably worse, she contracted polio. She had lost the use of her left leg by the time she was 6 years old.

A poor black family living in 1944 Clarksville, Tennessee, had no readily available medical treatments. Her brothers and sisters took turns massaging Wilma's crippled left leg every day. Twice a week, her mother, Blanche, a domestic worker, took her 50 miles each way on a bus to a Nashville hospital for blacks to get therapy. Years of massages, treatment, and a fierce determination to be a normal kid finally worked. Wilma slowly regained her mobility, graduating from crutches, to leg braces, to special high-top shoes, and finally to regular footwear. Six years after her bout of polio, she could walk normally again.

THE MAKING OF THE WORLD'S FASTEST WOMAN

Freed from her paralysis, Rudolph's natural talents shone through. She ran. Because she could. Because she finally could, she ran. She ran with such speed and with such skill that, by the time she was in high school, Rudolph had attracted the attention of one of Tennessee State University's track coaches, Ed Temple. He invited her to train with the team, the Tigerbelles. Great coaching, hard work, and the support of her teammates enabled Rudolph to unleash her potential and qualify for the 1956 Olympic Games in Melbourne. At the tender age of 16, 10 years after being crippled by polio, she won a bronze medal for the United States in the 4 × 100-meter relay. She reached her prime 4 years later, just in time for the 1960 Olympics in Rome.

Rudolph became the first American woman to win three gold medals in one Olympic Games. With her victories in the 100- and 200-meter sprints, she earned the title "the world's fastest woman." Rudolph also anchored the US team to victory in the relay, breaking records along the way.

Charismatic, beautiful, and charming, Rudolph became a sensation after the 1960 Olympics. Dubbed "The Black Pearl" and "The Black Gazelle" by newspapers, she was feted with parades and banquets around Europe and back in the United States.

As intoxicating as the fame was, Rudolph saw beyond it. She did the one essential thing that allows champions to break through to the next level of greatness. She kept growing and working for the well-being of others. "What do you do after you are world famous at 20 years old and have sat with prime ministers, kings, queens, and the Pope?" she wrote in her autobiography, *Wilma*. "You come back to the real world."

At that time, track and field was a thoroughly amateur sport. Since she couldn't earn a living from running, she retired from the sport 2 years after the Olympics, at age 22. Only then did she find her calling. Rather than grieving over the end of her athletic career, she established new goals. Rudolph became a teacher and women's track coach first at a high school and later at DePauw University in Indiana. From this platform, she was able to mentor hundreds of young people, providing the same kind of encouragement, support, and coaching that she received as a young woman.

Rudolph's influence reached beyond the girls she was coaching. In particular, she inspired young African American female athletes. Most notable was Florence Griffith Joyner, the next woman to win three gold medals in one Olympics, in 1988.

In 1982, she founded the Wilma Rudolph Foundation, a nonprofit, community-based amateur sports program to help disadvantaged children learn about hard work, dedication, and discipline in athletics and in life. She said that the foundation would be her greatest legacy. Rudolph died of a brain tumor at the young age of 54.

WHAT IS A LEGACY, ANYWAY?

The stages of The Dynamic Path through which this book has traveled have had one thing in common: They have had a clear and definable benefit for the individual traveling through them. With legacy building, that no longer holds. That isn't to say that there isn't a benefit here. In fact, the rewards that accrue from the creation of a lasting legacy probably outweigh all that come before. The benefits are, however, indefinable. What is it worth to change the world? How does one measure the influence to do great good? How can you assess or quantify immortality?

And yet, those who have amassed great wealth, great power, or great fame are remembered not for the achievements they racked up for themselves, but rather for the success they bestowed upon those they touched. If you do not hunger to do colossal good with the same fire you hunger for championship status or leadership position, you will never achieve it. The pyramid here is the narrowest of all. And, oddly enough, the drive that brings someone to the rarified place where he or she *can* leave a legacy must maintain its power, even as it changes itself utterly. No longer is the good of the individual paramount. The—there's no other word for it—selfish drive that propels championship individuals to positions of powerful leadership must become a selfless engine that works for the greater good.

MAINE'S NUMBER-ONE CITIZEN

An inspiring case of a champion who has transformed her effort for that greater good is Joan Benoit-Samuelson, a role model for women everywhere, especially in her home state. As Maine's first female athlete to achieve world renown, she has become an inspiring exemplar of dedication and excellence. When she began high school, only one in 27 girls in Maine participated in competitive high school sports. Today, thanks to Title IX, popular culture, and compelling role models like Benoit, the ratio is now one in three. She has channeled her energies and focus—her calling—into improving her beloved state. She has been a tireless leader in Maine's Big Brothers/Big Sisters program and with the Special Olympics, the Maine Women's Fund, and the Governor's Executive Council on Communities for Children. Most significantly to Benoit, in 1998, she fulfilled her dream of bringing a world-class road race to Maine by establishing the Beach to Beacon, a 10-kilometer race held in Cape Elizabeth each August. "I don't think there's a more beautiful backdrop than the Portland Head Light," she says, "which was the first lighthouse sited by George Washington." In a fitting tribute to her and to the Maine children's charities that the race benefits, many of the world's top distance runners have made the race a core part of their annual race schedules.

Benoit-Samuelson has long been driven to have an impact on others. "To me, life is all about giving back," she says. She does that by sharing her expertise through running clinics, coaching women's cross-country and long-distance running organizations, serving as a sports commentator and as a motivational speaker, and working to protect Maine's environment. "I've grown up on Casco Bay [at Portland], and we need to protect our natural resources," she says.

In a moment of self-reflection, however, she admits that at this point in her life she has some important decisions to make. "I'm at a turning point right now. I volunteer extensively and I feel like I'm making a real difference. But I don't want to volunteer my life away. I need to sink my teeth into something. What is it that I really want to do?" Benoit-Samuelson is working on finding a way to tie all of her experience and interests together in a way that makes sense, is economically viable (she has two college-age children), and is consistent with her core values of hard work, service, excellence, and determination.

That transformation from being a driven performer to working for the greater good would seem to be a straightforward, if challenging, path to follow. However, the drive to leave a legacy must be accompanied by the *skills* necessary to achieve it. You may not realize it, but the transition into personal leadership, with its attendant demands for blazing a moral and spiritual path for those you lead, is boot camp for legacy building. There is no school for this save the experience you gain wielding your influence for the good of those around you. As you transition into a legacy role, the success you inspire will no longer reflect directly upon you.

Doing pure good in the world may be nice, but it isn't what actually motivates most people. If it were, our mission-driven nonprofits would be overflowing with the nation's best and brightest. While I cast no aspersions on the quality of those who work to help others, the fact is that financial gain, power, and prestige have long attracted many of the most talented and ambitious in society, although happily, no small number also seek the same fulfillment in more altruistic pursuits.

How then does a leader muster the fire to leave a legacy? And why does this transition happen to the truly great again and again?

MAGIC

I remember the first time I ever saw Magic play basketball. The date was March 26, 1979, and the occasion was the championship game of the NCAA Final Four. It was one of the most memorable college basketball matchups ever: number-three ranked Michigan State, led by Earvin "Magic" Johnson, against number-one ranked, 33-0 Indiana State, led by Larry Bird. The game was a thriller. The Michigan State Spartans contained Bird with double and triple coverage while Magic lived up to his nickname with improbable passes and graceful, nothing-but-net shots from the field. Michigan State won the game by 11, 75 to 64, and Magic outscored Bird 24 to 19.

I suppose I wasn't the only one who first remembers seeing Magic play in that game. It was a made-for-television drama, and the game ended up being the most-watched NCAA championship game ever. He was named the tournament's most valuable player, and *Sports Illustrated* commemorated the achievement with the cover-story headline "The Magic Show."

Born on August 14, 1959, Earvin Johnson Jr. grew up in Lansing, Michigan, with nine brothers and sisters. His father worked in a General Motors plant, and his mother worked as a school custodian. As a boy, he would get on the court by 7:30 most mornings, often practicing all day long. A local sportswriter bestowed on him the name Magic when Earvin was a standout player at Everett High School. Johnson's mother, who was devoutly religious, loathed the nickname, thinking it blasphemous. It stuck despite her objections. Close-to-home Michigan State captured Magic for as long as the college stage could hold him.

By the time his junior year rolled around, Magic was destined for the NBA. He went on to achieve just about everything a player could dream of over the course of his 13-year NBA career, all of which was spent with the Los Angeles Lakers. He was a member of five NBA championship teams and won the league MVP and the finals MVP award three times each. Magic was a 12-time All-Star and a nine-time member of the All-NBA First Team. He scored a total of 17,707 points (19.5 points per game), made 6,559 rebounds (7.2 rebounds per game), and set an NBA record of 10,141 career assists (11.2 per game), a mark that was later surpassed by John Stockton. To cap it all off, he won a gold medal with the original Dream Team at the 1992 Olympics in Barcelona, Spain.

Magic dazzled fans and wrong-footed opponents with no-look passes off of fast breaks, laser-guided alley-oops from just inside the midcourt line, and spinning feeds driving to the basket through double and triple teaming. When opponents thought he was going to pass, he took a shot. When they expected him to shoot, he passed. But what Magic really passed along was exuberance and enthusiasm for the game.

Then just before the start of the 1991–92 season, Magic stunned the world.

REFUSING TO ACCEPT HIV AS A DEATH SENTENCE

On November 5, 1991, Magic was at a doctor's office in Los Angeles following up on a failed life-insurance examination. There were medical red flags going up all over, and when the doctor told him the diagnosis, he pulled no punches. Johnson had HIV. The doctor quickly added that he was done playing basketball and that he was soon going to die.

Two days of total disbelief and sheer disorientation followed. It didn't make any sense. He felt perfectly fine, as strong as ever, and had been all geared up for the season. He was hoping it was just a bad dream. But as he replayed his life in his mind, including a personal history of promiscuity, he slowly came to the realization that it wasn't just a bad dream. He had HIV and he was Magic Johnson. He concluded that he would have to deal with it the same way he had always dealt with other challenges—straight on.

On November 7, 1991, in a closed meeting with his fellow Lakers—players, coaches, and team management—followed by a press conference, Magic delivered the same somber message to both groups: He had contracted the virus that causes AIDS and was retiring. "Because of the HIV virus that I have attained," he announced at the Forum Club in Los Angeles on that day, "I will have to retire from the Lakers today. I do not have the AIDS disease. I plan on going on living for a long time, bugging you guys like I always have, so you'll see me around. I guess I now get to enjoy some of the other sides of living that I've missed." Grown men started bawling. But Magic was stoic the entire time, his voice never cracking, even maintaining a hint of his characteristic smile.

He then used the emotionally raw moment to lay the foundation for his life's calling. "I will now become a spokesman for HIV," he said. "I want people to realize that they should practice safe sex. Sometimes you are naive about it and think that it could never happen to you. It has happened and I'm going to deal with it. Sometimes we think only gay people can get it, or that it's not going to happen to me. Here I am, saying it can happen to anybody. Even me, Magic Johnson."

Some time later, in an interview with GQ magazine, Magic recalled that he felt that it was important at that time to step up and take responsibility and be a leader, a role his teammates had come to expect of him. "No matter what the situation," he said, "I had to be Earvin. I'm a calm person. I embrace challenges. This was another challenge in my life."

MJF AND MAGIC, THE BUSINESS LEADER

A month after the public announcement that he had contracted the virus, in December 1991, Johnson founded the Magic Johnson Foundation (MJF) dedicated to HIV/AIDS prevention and health care in inner-city communities. He wanted to create a structure for his desire to use his situation to help others. He was following the same advice given by Bill Bradley's coach years earlier—"Help others, help yourself." The foundation later broadened its mission to identify and support community-based organizations that address the educational, health, and social needs of children, young adults, and inner-city communities throughout the nation.

Johnson has worked tirelessly to educate the world about HIV/AIDS. He has spoken out about the need for and importance of HIV testing. His words and example have made it acceptable in minority communities, where cultures often run counter to testing in the first place and taking medication if the virus is detected, to get tested and to take medication when necessary.

His efforts have coincided with an amazing degree of medical advancements that have allowed people with HIV/AIDS to keep the disease at bay. In 1992, there was only one drug that treated the disease's progression. Today there are 26. With this explosion in medicine, the prices for the drugs have also fallen dramatically. As Magic has spoken out about the power of testing and early detection as well as the capabilities of combinations of drugs to prolong one's life, he has had an increasing effect on individuals, families, and communities struggling with the disease.

In 1993, while working hard on the war against HIV/AIDS, Johnson expanded his efforts into the business realm. He established Johnson Development Corporation (JDC) with the ambitious goal of creating successful commercial ventures that would revitalize economically depressed minority neighborhoods. JDC opened movie theaters and provided other quality entertainment services, creating desperately needed jobs and employing local minority contractors and service vendors. Magic teamed up with Howard Schultz, founder and chairman of Starbucks, to establish a 50-50 partnership between JDC and Starbucks Coffee Company to form Urban Coffee Opportunities (UCO). JDC is Starbucks' only partner to date in the United States.

Magic loves being a business leader, and it turns out that he is exceptionally good at it. He also believes in the concept of doing well by doing good, understanding the financial potential of empowering urban America, providing much-needed jobs to minorities, and developing underserved communities. As in the case of the joint venture with Starbucks, he is savvy about using his celebrity and the power of his social mission to attract the world's best and brightest to economic opportunities.

If it sounds extensive and exhaustive, it is. And it is only part of Magic's efforts. Would he have had the motivation and drive to achieve all of this without the adversity of the HIV diagnosis? Perhaps. But with that stimulus, Magic has channeled his extraordinary natural talents, dedication, and people leadership into a series of activities and programs that are creating a legacy even greater than his championship play over 13 seasons in the NBA. Up until 1991, he proved to the world that he could be highly successful in basketball. In the past 15 years, Johnson's extraordinary success demonstrates his positive power off the court as well.

How did Magic, in his darkest moment, summon the motivation to build a legacy? For one thing, he drew courage from his years of hard work on the basketball court, setting ambitious goals, pushing himself to exhaustion time and time again, and seeing the championship results that all of this achieved. Even more importantly, he came to recognize that as he began to work hard for the health and economic advancement of others, the process redounded to everyone's benefit, including his own. The harder he worked—speaking out about HIV/AIDS, working to influence relevant legislation, meeting with individuals and groups, and raising money, for example—the more he inspired others to believe and to work harder within the business and organizational structures Magic was building. The more productively people worked, the greater the positive impact on an increasingly large number of people and communities. This then cascaded back to Magic in the form of strength-giving positive reinforcement for his efforts, permitting him to continue his difficult and important work. From the very beginning of his new life after November 1991, Magic had a reason far greater than himself—a genuine calling—to fight to stay healthy for. Ever since, he has been fiercely dedicated to the medical and fitness regimens developed with his doctors and advisors to remain healthy. This in turn has enabled him to keep the virtuous cycle of his legacy building rolling firmly ahead.

THE BUILDING OF A LEGACY

In building a legacy, you need to live with integrity and live your life in a way that is consistent with your calling. To transform your calling into a legacy for others, the cause to which you're committed has to carry great weight for others while also being genuine to you. You need to have "permission" to own a cause for it to achieve a fundamental impact.

By *permission*, I mean people need to understand *why* you are drawn to a particular cause. It's about credibility. For example, when asked whether he has thought about supporting causes other than cancer, Lance Armstrong says, "Being a cancer survivor, it would be hard for me to go out and be the spokesperson for, say, juvenile diabetes. Not that that isn't a great organization." But while Lance has all the permission in the world to fight cancer, he has no credibility whatsoever for juvenile diabetes or many other extremely worthy causes.

When people buy into the rationale behind your calling, they also need to buy into *you* in order for them to embrace your cause fully. Millions wore the yellow "Livestrong" bracelet because they knew that it would contribute financially to cancer research and they respected the rationale for Lance's dedication. But they also wore it because they admired Lance as a person, identified with his dedication, and in most cases wanted to be more like him by wearing it.

The true legacy builder is a people leader, inspiring others to support a cause, and also a problem solver, showing people how *their* efforts can make an impact. Buy a "Livestrong" bracelet and a portion of the money finds its way to cancer research. Lance and the dedicated people working with him have figured out how a small action on your part can be a part of a much larger impact on their cause.

As in the case of the great champion in sports or the invaluable business professional at work, the foundational component of greatness remains a sustained level of hard work and commitment. Based on all of my research, it is clear that legacy builders work just as hard in this stage of their lives as they did earlier in their careers, even though the kind of work they do has shifted from directed practice to things like public speaking, strategy sessions, alliance development, and fund-raising. They also exercise the mental discipline and courage to adapt to the changing world and maintain a sustained focus on making others around them successful. Do this and you too will continue to grow as a leader and person. The dynamics involved in building a legacy are less about you and your own talents and more about moving others to action. As you pursue your calling and direct your attention and energies and those of others toward making a positive impact, your moral and spiritual leadership will expand accordingly, as illustrated in the final chart below, "Composition of a Legacy Builder."

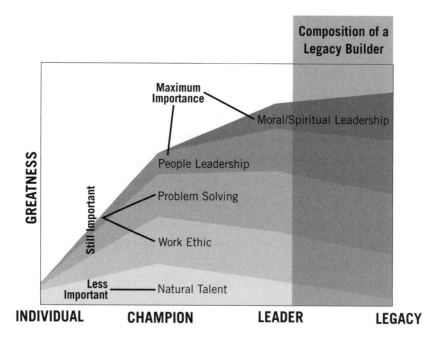

THE MAN IN THE ORANGE SUNGLASSES

He is one of the most recognizable human beings on the planet. With his signature orange-lensed sunglasses, silver hoop earring, and 3-day stubble, everyone from music fans, to finance ministers and heads of state, to suffering people across Africa feels connected to Bono. The Irish musician, diplomat, and philanthropist has transcended the world of rock music to become a driving force in global economic policy and a world leader in the war against AIDS in Africa.

Bono's transformation from pop star to global colossus has lessons for anyone ready to embark on the final step of The Dynamic Path.

Bono is indeed a powerful role model, due in large part, of course, to the impact he makes through his dedicated efforts around the world. But there is another lesson to be drawn from Bono's example as well. That is to make the *absolute most* out of the hand that you've been dealt. Given your own natural talents and the context of your work and life, it's never too soon—or too late—to reflect on how you can apply your capabilities to making a positive impact on others. Do that and you will take a meaningful step toward building a legacy.

Personally, I don't think I've ever met anyone who so thoroughly utilizes his skills and station in life as Bono. He has gone from recording artist to global conscience by leveraging his fame, access, credibility, and basic skill sets—writing, recording, and performing music, popularizing words and concepts, and applying a stunning intellect and prodigious energy level—to allow drowned-out voices to be heard.

WHO *IS* BONO?

Born Paul Hewson in 1960, Bono was raised by a Catholic father and a Protestant mother in Dublin's middle class. He was a highly intelligent boy, competing in international chess tournaments at the age of 12.

When he was 14, Bono's beloved mother suddenly died, leaving him to be raised by a single father and older brother. He turned away from family and school and, seeking refuge in music, began playing with his local buddies. In 1976, when he was 16, Bono and his friends started a band that they called U2.

Bono had experienced just enough suffering to give a sharp edge to his music but not so much that it extinguished his underlying optimism. Bono's engaging, animating spirit connected U2's performances, words, and melodies with the band's audiences.

Amazingly, the members of U2 have all been together ever since the band's founding. Just as a 30-year run with one company is rare in the corporate world, it is almost unheard of in the music business. But in the case of U2, even the band's manager has been with them from the very start. To a greater or lesser extent, all of the members of U2 side-stepped serious alcohol and drug problems, and that has played an important role in the band's longevity. However, even more important was a decision they all agreed upon at the beginning—to share revenue equally among all of the band's members. In other bands, Bono and the Edge, the lead guitarist, could have claimed songwriting revenue and a greater percentage of the gross. But because they were all friends and commercial interests were the secondary objective of the band, they turned their back on this convention. "All of us want our lives to count," Bono says. "Music for me was always about changing the world."

From the very beginning, U2 has been committed to addressing important issues facing the world. Starting in the early 1980s, every tour had a cause-related sponsor—Greenpeace, Amnesty International, and Nelson Mandela, to name a few. In 1985, U2 played at the Live Aid concert to raise money for Ethiopia, then in the grip of a powerful famine and struggling under the weight of huge indebtedness to Western nations. While U2's participation wasn't unique—just about every other major band also played the festival—what was different was that Bono worked hard to understand the real problem they were rallying about. He and his wife, Ali (whom he met at age 12 and started dating at 16), traveled to Ethiopia later that year and spent several months living and working in a refugee camp.

From there Bono's road diverged further from that of the many other well-intentioned celebrities across the international entertainment landscape. While others made cameo appearances and public service announcements, Bono dove into the economics and policy-making apparatus of debt relief. Never shy about leveraging his fame for access to the most influential people, Bono secured meetings with the leaders of the global financial community. He also met with the world's most powerful international development economist, Jeffrey D. Sachs, who was then at Harvard University and has been an economics professor and director of the Earth Institute at Columbia University since 2002.

The result of this educational extravaganza was Bono's campaign to cancel 100 percent of the $6 billion that the poorest African nations, including Ethiopia, owed the United States. The Clinton administration had already forgiven two-thirds of this amount, but Bono argued that you can't tap into people's emotions and imaginations without tackling the whole thing. "You can't sing about two-thirds of something," he said.

Bono put hundreds of hours into the debt-relief effort over the course of 2000. He traveled to Washington eight times and met with key legislators and their staffs. He even went so far as to enlist clergy members in the home district of a reluctant Alabama congressman to sermonize about debt relief on Sunday mornings. The result, in no small part due to Bono's leadership, was a $435 million congressional grant for 100 percent debt relief.

Bono sought to build on the momentum resulting from his work on debt relief. Energized by the positive reinforcement of making genuine progress, coupled with the intoxicating level of respect proffered to him by world leaders, he approached Bill Gates and others to provide financing for broader action on Africa. This gave way to a nonprofit advocacy organization called DATA that Bono founded in 2002 along with philanthropist, record producer, and friend (and member of the Kennedy clan) Bobby Shriver. DATA, which stands for Debt, AIDS, Trade, Africa, has been committed to addressing the three issues that underlie the most serious problems on the African continent—unpayable debts, the spread of AIDS, and harmful trade policies—by raising public awareness and working with government leaders in the industrialized world to bring more resources to the region.

(RED)

If you've noticed a proliferation of fashion-forward consumer products recently that all share a deep crimson hue, you're not alone. That would be the latest product of Bono's creative energies. Red Apple iPod, Red Motorola RAZR, Red Gap Jeans, American Express Red Card—these are some of the iconic brands that have signed on to become partners in Product (RED).

Founded by Bono and Bobby Shriver in 2006, Product (RED) is an innovative for-profit approach to attacking the issue of fighting AIDS in Africa. Just as he did with debt relief, Bono went to school on the science and pharmacology of HIV and the AIDS epidemic. Healthcare experts who have met Bono frequently comment that he knows as much as any scientific journal editor about the critical medical issues. And when Bono speaks about Product (RED), his insights about marketing budgets, consumer demand, and the business model are as sound as those of any chief executive or venture capitalist.

"AIDS is no longer a death sentence," Bono says. "Just two pills a day will bring someone who is at death's door back to a full life. These pills, which are available at the corner drugstore, cost less than a dollar a day.

But since the poorest people in Africa earn less than a dollar a day, they can't afford to buy the medicine and so they die, at the alarming rate of 6,500 people a day. It's unnecessary," Bono says. "It's insane."

Bono says that a key part of his motivation for selecting the issue of AIDS in Africa, beyond having personally spent time there connecting deeply with real people suffering from the disease, is that "it is an entirely winnable war." The medicine is inexpensive and readily available. People want to help, even though they aren't necessarily prepared to go out of their way or spend extra money to do so. Companies would like to wrap their brands into the conscientious consumerism that is driving billions of dollars of purchasing power, but competition and shareholder activism are so acute they can't afford to make meaningful corporate contributions to even the most important causes. However, if consumers can go about their normal lives and make purchasing choices that meet their needs while appealing to their conscience and desire to help, and companies can win more profitable business that more than funds their contributions, and people in Africa can receive the medicine to treat HIV/AIDS, then you create a win-win-win.

That is an example of Bono's genius. If he weren't a rock star and diplomatic world changer, he easily could have been a great chief executive. He leads by example. No one works harder or delves more deeply into issues and data than he does. He surrounds himself with the best people, is an extraordinary listener, and takes advice extremely well. He understands economics, markets, consumers, media, science, government, and regulation. And he has a dynamism that attracts and inspires just about everyone he meets.

If a single individual with a sharp mind, a gift for writing a catchy melody and memorable lyric, a dynamic personality, and a genuine desire to make the world a better place can have such a far-reaching and positive impact, it makes one wonder what *you* can do.

Archie Griffin—
The Three Ds: Desire, Dedication, and Determination

"He's a better young man than he
is a football player, and he's the
best football player I've ever seen."

Legendary Ohio State Football Coach
Woody Hayes on Archie Griffin

Archie Griffin, the only two-time Heisman Trophy winner ever, could have made millions from his success on the football field. Instead, he chose to live a life of service to the university he loves, Ohio State, and to the thousands of student athletes who go through the OSU system. In 19 years, he rose to become Ohio State's associate director of athletics. In this role, he oversaw 17 men's and women's varsity sports, including, of course, football. In 2004, he moved to a new challenge, becoming president of the Ohio State Alumni Association, the second largest such association (behind Penn State).

Griffin is one of the most celebrated names in Ohio State's rich football lore. A three-time all-American between 1973 and 1975, he made college football history by becoming the first and only two-time winner of the Heisman Trophy. He received the coveted bronze statue in 1974 as a junior and again in 1975 as a senior. The only Big Ten player ever to start in four Rose Bowls, he rushed for an Ohio State record of 5,589 yards and helped the Buckeyes capture four Big Ten titles and post an overall record of 40-5-1.

"When I was growing up," Griffin says, "my parents instilled our values and priorities. First was a strong belief in God. Second was the importance of education and, in particular, a college education. The third priority was to participate in sports. They felt that playing sports rounds you out as an individual and teaches you life lessons such as the will to win, dealing with pressure, and getting along in a team situation. Most importantly, sports, and football especially, teaches you to get up after you get knocked down." These priorities were not bestowed upon Archie uniquely, but on his six brothers and one sister as well. Griffin recalls the sacrifice that his father made to support his children. "I'll never forget that when I was in high school, my dad worked three jobs. He was a city sanitation worker, he worked for the Ohio Malleable Steel Casting Company, and he also had a custodial job. On Friday nights he would take vacation time in order to go and see his kids play football. At the time I didn't know this, but when I found out later that he cared so much to take vacation to come and watch us play, it made a dramatic impression on me." Not only did Archie go on to OSU glory, all six of his brothers went on to college and to play football as well.

Aside from his parents, another major influence on Griffin growing up was a man named Oscar Gill, a counselor to the student government, of which Griffin was president, at Lynmore Junior High School in Columbus, Ohio. "I remember him sitting us down and talking to us about three words, the Three Ds: Desire, Dedication, and Determination. From that point in time, those three words stuck with me, and I think about and use them all the time. With desire you have to have a goal in life, something to shoot for. Dedication gives you the commitment to achieve that goal. And determination enables you to overcome the obstacles that get in your way. Those three Ds have pretty much been my motto."

What impact did College Football Hall of Fame Coach Woody Hayes have on Griffin? "Coach Hayes left a legacy, for me and for all of the players who played under him. Even though he was notoriously tough and demanding, his emphasis was always on helping others. This led my wife and me to set up the Columbus Foundation, which is dedicated to helping children here in our community, and the Archie Griffin Scholarship Fund, through which I help young people get a college education."

This exemplifies how Griffin believes anyone can strive to create meaning in their life, even if they don't happen to be endowed with the skills to become a world-class athlete. "The way to build a legacy is through helping others," Griffin says. "I've been fortunate to have parents that led me the right way, and one of the things that they have always wanted me to do is set a good example not only for my kids, but for other kids as well. I don't think there's any better way to create a legacy or to feel better about your life than to help other people."

THE TRAILHEAD OF THE DYNAMIC PATH

While a legacy can take many forms, it is always based on one thing: an extension of you—your drive, your leadership, your essence—into the lives of others. A legacy is, ultimately, about leverage. You are leveraging your experience, your prestige, your power, your energy, your values, and your relationships to attack at least one of the world's multitude of problems. If that's a challenge that appeals to you, if it's *the* challenge that consumes your focus, then you will have arrived at the trailhead of The Dynamic Path. The way is no longer marked; with every step from here, you'll be breaking new terrain.

As you unlock your own true talents and apply your creative energies to the fullest, you can become one of those rare individuals who continues to grow over the course of his or her life and career through a focus beyond the first person. As you dedicate yourself to pursuing your calling and doing something meaningful in the world, you will be able to achieve your ultimate potential and earn the honor of building a legacy.

CHAPTER 10

Conclusion
Living the Dynamic Life

You're at a crossroads, and we're here to help.

While these nine words could be an apt way to summarize this book, I originally wrote them for an entirely different purpose and at another point in time. It was early 2002, and we were preparing for a major new business presentation. Going up against three other leading executive search firms, we were competing for the CEO search for a high-profile Internet company, Space.com, founded by CNN anchor Lou Dobbs. Among the impressive array of board directors who would be in the midtown Manhattan boardroom evaluating the presentation was none other than the first person to walk on the moon, Neil Armstrong. One important piece of advice that the director who invited Spencer Stuart to the pitch told me was "Don't, under any circumstances, ask Neil for his autograph. He never gives them, and there will be no more certain way to lose."

Oh well, I thought, it will still be cool to meet him.

To position our search strategy during the meeting, we presented an analysis of the Space.com situation. The company had a series of major strengths, such as the most heavily trafficked space-related Web site, a blue-chip roster of investors and directors, and the leading consumer astronomy software business, Starry Night. But the company also confronted serious challenges, such as a stretched balance sheet, a limited number of media platforms—Web, a newspaper, magazine, and software—and a very small size relative to other nonfiction/science-related media companies, such as Discovery Communications and National Geographic, which both had powerful television networks to provide programming and to spread out the large costs of content development. With the opportunity to bring in a new CEO (Lou Dobbs was returning to CNN full-time after taking a leave to run Space.com), the company could either build on its strengths, address its weaknesses, and thrive, or squander its advantages and succumb to its difficulties. It was at a crossroads.

Were we taking a risk asserting that the company was at a crossroads, the key premise on which our entire presentation was based? How did we know that the board would agree?

Happily, the board agreed that they *were* at a crossroads and that indeed we were the best team to help. So not only did we win the pitch (and go on to recruit a stellar CEO named Dan Stone, who has grown the company and renamed it Imaginova), but we came to the recognition that indeed any company is virtually always at a crossroads.

This realization also applies to each of us. Just as is the case with a company, any person is at a crossroads at any point in time. You are always at a crossroads when you travel along The Dynamic Path. The moment you realize that you have a choice to make, you are at a dynamic moment, deciding whether to focus on making money and getting by or on the more challenging journey toward achieving greatness as a champion, leader, or legacy builder.

ENTER BUZZ ALDRIN, THE *SECOND* MAN ON THE MOON

Despite having never been a competitive athlete, Buzz Aldrin's life has been significant and utterly dynamic. He is, perhaps, a nearly perfect example of The Dynamic Path, complete with its pitfalls and rewards. He became a true champion, confronted momentous difficulties, struggled through a series of dynamic moments, and found the strength to overcome them, going on to build a legacy for the benefit of the world. Moreover, since he did all of this through science, the military, NASA, and other organizations outside of sports and business, his story shows that The Dynamic Path can be equally valid across sectors and disciplines.

Edwin Eugene Aldrin was born January 20, 1930, in Montclair, New Jersey. But when his sister, Fay Ann, tried to call him "brother," all she could manage to say was "Buzzer." That got shortened to "Buzz," and no one ever called him anything else. Perhaps his lunar exploration was preordained: His mother's maiden name was Moon. His father, a colonel in the US Army during World War II, was a pilot in the Army Air Corps. After the war, he had a job with Standard Oil that took him all over the country, and he flew his own single-propeller Lockheed plane from one location to another. When Buzz was 2 years old, his father took him flying for the first time.

Though never a renowned athlete, Buzz enjoyed sports growing up. He swam, played pickup football, and pole-vaulted on the high school track team. No matter what the sport, Buzz had a strong drive to win and was known as a tough competitor.

After graduating from Montclair High School, Buzz wanted to be in the Air Force. He concluded that going to the US Military Academy at West Point would be his best route. At the academy, he followed every order and studied brutally hard, and by the end of his first year, he was first in his class. He ultimately graduated third in his class in 1951, which allowed him to select any assignment in the military. He kept true to his goal and joined the Air Force. Buzz learned, at long last, to fly fighter jets and exalted in the speed and feeling of breaking free from gravity. During the Korean War, he flew 66 combat missions.

He was stationed in Germany at the war's end, as a pilot testing supersonic planes. Seven men had been selected to fly a lot faster—they were America's first astronauts in the Mercury program, with the goal of orbiting the Earth. A West Point friend named Ed White told him that he was applying to the space program. Buzz realized that he could be a part of that too.

While Buzz was an excellent pilot, he was not at all unique relative to other strong candidates. To differentiate himself and become more valuable to the program, he decided to go back to school and become expert in a highly specialized segment of aeronautics. At the Massachusetts Institute of Technology, he studied the phenomenon of bringing different objects together in space, known as the rendezvous, which would be necessary for long-term missions in space. Whereas computers (even the rudimentary models of that time, which had less computing power than today's laptops) could do all of the calculations necessary for the rendezvous, Buzz believed that astronauts would need to understand it all themselves in case something went wrong. He earned his doctorate at MIT; his thesis was "Guidance for Manned Orbital Rendezvous."

Flush with confidence, he applied to the astronaut program. But to his astonishment, he was rejected. Hadn't he done everything "right"? While he was devastated by the setback—he felt that he had been preparing for this for his entire life—he let his mind rather than his emotions guide him. He kept an outward calm and an inner resolve and applied again. Assessing what had gone wrong the first time, he determined that he hadn't sufficiently emphasized the *unique* combination of his fighter pilot, test pilot, and scientific credentials. The second time around, he prevailed.

Buzz was ecstatic to become a member of the third group of astronauts named by NASA. His first spaceflight was on November 11, 1966, aboard Gemini 12. His mission, with Jim Lovell, was to orbit the Earth and to practice rendezvous techniques with another craft in space. Traveling in space at 17,500 miles per hour, it took them less than 2 hours to travel around the world. This was the flight that brought the Gemini program to a successful close.

The next program was Apollo, the mission that would put human beings on the Moon. When it was time for Apollo 11, the flight that would land on the Moon, Neil Armstrong, Mike Collins, and Buzz were next in line for flight. The day toward which they had worked so long and hard finally arrived on July 16, 1969, when Apollo 11 launched. President Kennedy's legendary 1961 challenge to the nation was soon to be achieved. Four days after launch, after traveling 240,000 miles, the three astronauts were in orbit around the Moon. On July 20, 1969, their spacecraft separated into two parts: Columbia, in which Mike Collins would remain in orbit, and the Eagle, the craft that would take Neil Armstrong and Buzz Aldrin to the Moon's surface and back up to Columbia.

As they descended toward the lunar surface, they looked out of the window at the spot the computer had chosen for the Eagle to land and saw that it was too rocky. In a split-second decision, they concluded they would have to control the Eagle themselves. Armstrong took control while Buzz used visual sight to let him know how far they were from the ground—200 feet, 100 feet, 40 feet. Talk about mental toughness in high-pressure moments. How did Buzz control his fear and anxiety during this time? "Well, the anxiousness was certainly there," Buzz recalls, "but the fear was not." He says that fear is a "mind-clouding emotion. You learn that as you go through jet pilot training." By the time the Eagle landed, they had used up almost all of their fuel; they had had only about 20 seconds left to spare.

Buzz says that he and Neil grinned at each other; there was nothing to say, and it was time to exit the Eagle. Armstrong climbed out first and descended the ladder to the surface of the Moon. The whole world, listening in, heard the famous words: "That's one small step for man, one giant leap for mankind." Buzz climbed down the ladder and joined Armstrong. He says that there was no color on the Moon; everything was either gray or white with the blackest sky above punctuated by the blue planet Earth—"home." Buzz took the American flag out of the storage cylinder, and together he and Armstrong forced the pole into the surface. Then Buzz and Neil Armstrong set down the plaque that would remain on the Moon:

HERE MEN FROM THE PLANET EARTH

FIRST SET FOOT UPON THE MOON

JULY 1969, A.D.

WE CAME IN PEACE FOR ALL MANKIND

LIFE AFTER WALKING ON THE MOON

When he returned from the historic mission, Buzz embarked on an international goodwill tour and was presented with the Presidential Medal of Freedom plus more than 50 distinguished awards from numerous countries of the world. He remained with NASA for 2 more years before resigning in July 1971. Over his space career, Buzz logged 289 hours and 53 minutes in space—7 hours and 52 minutes of which were spent in the Eagle.

But after the celebrations all died down, new challenges set in. Buzz was left with a giant void after accomplishing a singular goal that had consumed him for so many years. His situation was hardly unique—how to deal with having achieved a lifelong goal—even if the circumstances were. How many of us can chalk our sense of dislocation up to having seen our magnificent planet from the Moon, only to return to the Vietnam War, the civil rights struggles, and Watergate? He had no clear road map for how to live his life.

"Following my retirement from NASA and then the Air Force," Buzz said, "I had to deal with some things that cost me a decade of productivity. I had to recover from depression and alcoholism in many different treatment facilities." But with a lot of help and determination, he fought through his substance abuse and pulled himself together enough to find a new focus and pursue it with passion. "Now that I have had 27 years of sobriety, it has made me far more productive, imaginative, and creative than I ever was as an Air Force person or astronaut. Certainly I was more productive than [when] trying to reorient my life after leaving the very structured fields that were my career.

"I had to carve out my own path while I was trying to put my life back together again," Buzz added. One thing he did was to write. He wrote what he thinks is one of the best science fiction stories ever written as well as a children's book about his life as a boy and growing up to become an astronaut. Given that his whole life was geared toward space, it is only logical that this is where he would find his calling once again. He dedicated himself to ensuring a continued leading role for America in manned space exploration. To support his lifelong commitment to humans venturing outward in space, he founded a rocket design company, Starcraft Boosters, and the ShareSpace Foundation, a nonprofit organization devoted to pursuing space tourism. In addition, similar to Colin Powell, Buzz worked to create a portfolio of activities including not only writing, but lecturing around the world about ideas for exploring the universe and working on an alliance to use space and aviation to drive American education in math and the sciences.

Where does Buzz Aldrin go from here? "In 10 or 15 years, I'll sit back in my wheelchair and write all my memories in another book," he says with a smile. "But for now, I have strategic plans for how we travel to Mars. So I've got my hands full."

Full indeed.

AN INTIMATE DECLARATION

Every year for the past decade I have made a resolution intended to redress one of my greatest professional and personal shortcomings: being late. If this sounds relatively trivial, just ask anyone who works with me, or worse, ask my family. They wouldn't say it is so benign. It wreaks havoc with their busy schedules. It implies that I believe my time is more valuable than theirs. It is frustrating and disrespectful. My rationalization has always been "Well, even if I am 15 minutes late [it is usually worse than that], I am accomplishing so many things in those extra minutes that it's worth the cost." I had even come to believe that when it comes to time management, I have the equivalent of a learning disability.

Like the perpetual dieter or nicotine patch wearer, my efforts to improve this deplorable behavior have gone for naught.

Until now. At the risk of sounding corny and subjecting myself to eternal scrutiny, I can honestly say that by applying the lessons of The Dynamic Path, I am finally cracking the code. The early returns from the changes that I have been making have already provided a glimpse into a long-term payoff that far surpasses any conceivable expectation: reduced stress, less guilt, greater productivity, and improved relationships.

What exactly have I been doing? I'll start with what I've *not* been doing: trying to work harder to fit more tasks into a fixed amount of time, multitasking more, or sleeping less.

Here's what I did do, drawn right from the pages of this book. I have:

▶ Created a concrete goal: The schedule is *paramount.*

▶ Established a mantra to keep focused on what I can control: Today's schedule is more important than yesterday's tardiness.

▶ Controlled distractions: Pay attention and be "fully present" in meetings, conference calls, and in time with friends and family.

▶ Assessed my performance at the end of each day: What commitments was I on time for and why? What commitments was I late for and why? What am I going to do differently tomorrow?

▶ Decoupled my punctuality from my quality as a person: Being late does not make me a bad person; yes, it's disrespectful, but I'm working on addressing it, so if anything, it makes me a good person.

As I become more skilled in the thought processes of the mind of a champion, better and more consistent in the deliberate practice at the core of my professional work, even more committed to the success of those around me, and more focused on pursuing the causes that compose my calling, I feel that I am very much living the dynamic life.

You are at a crossroads, and we are here to help.
Whether you recognize it or not, you're at a crossroads all the time. No matter what's happening at this point in your life, if you choose to do so, you can climb aboard and pursue The Dynamic Path. Regardless of each of our circumstances—rich or poor, young or old—we will all confront grave disappointments, inevitable setbacks, and momentous turning points. We will have to make difficult decisions among sub-optimal alternatives with no one there to tell us what we should do. Any moment we pause for a decision is in itself a dynamic moment. The most exasperating part of The Dynamic Path is its very dynamism: You must choose every moment to be on it. To shirk that choice is to step off the path. Then you, like Buzz or like me, will need to claw your way back on. But the path is always there, always ready to be walked.

It's now over to you. Decide.

Appendix

Discipline, Dynamics, and Manned Flight
Intellectual Exploration of Dynamics

Beginning in the 1970s, on NBC's *Saturday Night Live*, comedian Don Novello portrayed Father Guido Sarducci, a Vatican emissary who postulated that everything one needed to know could be learned at the Five-Minute University. "In the Five Minute University," he explained, "Spanish is reduced to the phrases, 'Como—está—usted?' and '*Muy*—bien.' All you need to know about economics," he added, "is 'Supply—and demand!' Theology," he concluded, "is simply, 'God is everywhere.'"

In an ode to the Five-Minute University, let's take a brief dive into the world of dynamics: defining it, exploring its etymology, and observing its application across a variety of situations over time.

DYNAMIC \ Dī 'NA MIK \ ADJ. CHARACTERIZED BY ACTION OR FORCEFULNESS OR FORCE OF PERSONALITY; PERTAINING TO ENERGY OR PRODUCTION OF FORCE.
Source: *Webster's Revised Unabridged Dictionary (1913)*

The word *dynamic* is powerful, both literally and figuratively. The individual who coined the term "dynamic" was Gottfried Leibniz, the German mathematician and philosopher. Leibniz is best known in mathematics as the inventor of calculus and in philosophy for the idea of optimism. In 1691, he introduced the word *dynamisch*, drawing on the Greek word *dynamikos*, meaning powerful.

Dynamics as a branch of physics, in the sense of "force producing motion," came into use in 1788. By 1856, according to linguistic historians, *dynamism* took on the figurative meaning of "active; potent; energetic." From that point, over the past $1\frac{1}{2}$ centuries, dynamics has been subdivided into many different branches, from group dynamics to aerodynamics and many things in between. In 2006, Microsoft even launched a new line of software and a supporting marketing campaign heralding the message that "There are infinite dynamics in business. Master them all. With Microsoft Dynamics." The position of the word *dynamics* in contemporary life and culture can be readily described with a single number: 744 million. This is the number of hits yielded by a Google search.

DISCIPLINE, DYNAMICS, AND MANNED FLIGHT

On December 17 at Kitty Hawk, North Carolina, Orville Wright and his older brother Wilbur succeeded in making the first sustained powered flight in an aircraft heavier than air. Their world-altering accomplishment took advantage of many different forms of dynamics over a 15-year period that culminated one crisp morning in 1903 on the blustery beaches of North Carolina. It was the end result of channeling the powers of thermodynamics, aerodynamics, fluid dynamics, and even group dynamics to attack their singular goal—achieving manned flight.

Their path began 25 years earlier when Orville was a 7-year-old boy and Wilbur was 11. In 1878, their father, Milton Wright, gave the boys a present, a toy helicopter designed by a man named Alphonse Penaud, a French experimenter who was well ahead of his time. The helicopter's rubber-spring-driven rotor lifted the craft into the air and fascinated the boys so much that they built a number of copies of the toy. The skills that would help get them into flight years later were in early evidence as their models successfully took flight. The boys hoped one day to build a helicopter large and powerful enough to send their bodies and not just their imaginations into the air.

While adulthood brought a more practical line of work as owners of a bicycle shop in their hometown of Dayton, Ohio, flying remained firmly implanted in their minds. As the turn of the century approached, bicycles were at the cutting edge of transportation technology. The brothers recognized that riding a bike, which is based on balance and speed, was about as close as they could get to flying until they figured out how to become airborne.

Beginning in 1890, they followed news reports about a German engineer who was experimenting with gliders. Six years later, the report of his tragic death revived a more active interest in manned flight in Wilbur and Orville.

The Wright brothers were both disciplined and creative in their quest for knowledge about flight. Wilbur wrote a letter to the Smithsonian Institution, which at that time was the center of what little research was being done in aeronautics. He requested "such papers as the Smithsonian Institution has published on aeronautics," as well as a list of "other works in print in the English language." Wilbur was able to work through the boxes of material with the rigor of an engineer and the logical problem-solving skills of a trial attorney. Before long, he was able to reduce the problem of manned flight to three discrete requirements: (1) wings to provide lift; (2) a power source to move the aircraft forward with enough speed to create sufficient air to flow over the wings to generate the lift; and (3) a means to control the aircraft. Straightforward as this list was, no one yet working on flight had reduced the problem to these concrete areas. Wilbur's studies of the preexisting research unearthed physics equations and data that helped him and Orville design wings and determine how much velocity was needed to generate the necessary lift, and how powerful an engine would have to be to achieve this speed.

No others had yet addressed how to create controls for the aircraft that would enable them to fly safely, avoiding the fate of the doomed German glider pioneer. To attack this vexing problem, the brothers returned to the idea that flight was somewhat akin to the activity around which their vocation was based—riding a bicycle. As any parent who has run next to and ultimately behind a young child knows, the only way to learn how to ride a bike is to . . . ride a bike. Similarly, the Wrights realized that rather than relying on data and analysis to determine how to control an aircraft, they needed the practical experience of flying to learn how to fly and control an aircraft.

Before risking their lives, the Wright brothers needed to come up with a method to achieve control of an aircraft. Where did they look for inspiration? To the sky, of course. In extensive observation of how birds manage to fly, Wilbur determined that they do more than just shift their weight to maintain control. They achieve and sustain equilibrium by turning the edge of one wing tip up and the other down. This subtle but seminal insight gave the brothers the impetus to design wings that could be twisted in a controlled manner.

With the problem of control essentially solved, they set about building a kite with a 5-foot wingspan that was a scale model of a plane, whose wings could be twisted by the kite flier pulling on different strings. In August 1899, the brothers succeeded in flying and controlling the model plane. Now it was only a matter of scaling up the model into a vehicle large enough for one of them to fly.

But they quickly hit a roadblock—wind. The brothers calculated that they needed to find a location where the winds blew consistently at about 15 miles per hour. Wilbur contacted the United States Weather Bureau for a list of candidate locations. In reviewing the list provided by the bureau, he concluded that Kitty Hawk, North Carolina, was the ideal place. Not only did it meet the requirement of sustained winds, it offered isolation to protect against prying eyes, dunes high enough to launch from, and the relatively soft landing of a beach in the not unlikely case of a crash landing.

So in the fall of 1900 the brothers set off for Kitty Hawk with their first-generation plane. It was a giant biplane kite with a 17-foot wingspan. It did not have an engine, but would fly on the wind. After repeated attempts to operate it as an unmanned kite, they completed their tests, climbed aboard, and successfully got airborne.

The next step was to build a more sophisticated glider aircraft that could sustain flight, which they did back in their Ohio workshop. When they returned to Kitty Hawk in 1901, however, they met with grave disappointment. The glider flew, but not nearly as long or as well as they had predicted based on their calculations. The wings provided just a fraction of the lift that was projected by the numbers. This setback was especially severe because they had long been working under the assumption that the only problem area left for them to solve was that of controlling the aircraft. Other inventors and engineers already had published reports describing the fluid dynamics and aerodynamics with supporting data. But when crunch time came, the data and the actual experience were sorely in opposition with one another. When they departed for Ohio from Kitty Hawk on August 21, 1901, Wilbur concluded despondently, "Not within a thousand years would man ever fly."

That was very nearly the end of the story. No one knows whether or when manned flight would have been discovered had a fortuitous event not occurred. Some months after returning to Ohio, Wilbur received a prestigious invitation to address the Chicago-based Western Society of Engineers. Motivated by a desire to perform well in front of a collective group of his peers, Wilbur reviewed in great detail the successes and failures of their past 2 years of aeronautical experiments. In the process of preparing his speech, he uncovered a massive disconnect between the performance projected by the numbers and the actual performance. He realized that there was nothing wrong with the equations or principles of aeronautics after all. Rather, he realized that he had relied on data supplied by others for the all-important coefficient of air pressure, which had not been confirmed with empirical evidence through experimentation.

The old saying "Necessity is the mother of invention" probably came into play at this point. What resulted was another breakthrough that was almost as significant as the airplane itself. They had to determine a way to figure out the coefficient figure accurately, but they did not want to venture back across the country by train and out to the beaches of Kitty Hawk to conduct tests. So they came up with an idea: to create a wind tunnel in the back of their bicycle shop for performing experiments. This appealed greatly to the introverted and data-driven brothers. In the privacy of their shop, they were able to test, read the results, and adjust, over and over again, all the way to figuring out how to design and build the most efficient wing.

What resulted was a glider with significantly longer and narrower wings, sleeker surface materials, and improved controls. When they tested the new and improved aircraft at Kitty Hawk in October 1902, the results were astounding. They recorded a flight of 622.5 feet that lasted for 26 seconds. They were now ready to install an engine.

Wilbur, ever the engineer, reduced the problem of power to two components, force and weight. He calculated that they needed to find an engine that would generate 8 to 9 horsepower and weigh less than 180 pounds. The brothers sent inquiries to 10 engine manufacturers, but not a single one had a motor that small, nor did any have an interest in developing one for a nonexistent market. So, once again, the Wright brothers had to figure it out for themselves. They found a talented local machinist, and together they designed and built a motor that ended up weighing 200 pounds but generated 12 horsepower.

There was one final element that was needed before they were ready to fly—a propeller. This turned out to be just one more thing that had no precedent. The brothers had assumed that since shipbuilders had had centuries of experience with fluid dynamics, there would be a strong theoretical basis that governed the design of marine propellers that they could adapt to air. But that was not at all the case. Until that point in time, ship propellers were designed based on nautical tradition rather than principles and theory. So Wilbur again got to work, clearly energized by the challenge. Applying the learning from all of their efforts in wing design, Wilbur discovered that the propeller was no more than an airplane wing travelling in a spiral course pulling the aircraft through the air (as opposed to a "screw" that pushed a ship through water).

The table was finally set to venture back to Kitty Hawk to put it all together and achieve manned flight. The first effort on December 14, with Wilbur as pilot, was a failure. The craft stalled and fell to the ground almost immediately. After 2 days of repairs, it was Orville's turn. And so it was, on the morning of December 17, 1903, when the wind was just right, that Orville launched and successfully covered 120 feet while remaining aloft for 12 seconds. The brothers kept at it over the course of that historic first day of flight. By the fourth and final launch, Wilbur flew 852 feet in 59 seconds.

DYNAMICS IN ACTION

What does the Wright brothers' incredible story tell us about dynamics? Let's take a look.

Fluid Dynamics and Aerodynamics

The first and most obvious place to see dynamics at work in the Wright brothers' quest for manned flight clearly is in the effect of fluid dynamics. This is the discipline that studies fluids, both liquids and gases, in motion. Fluid dynamics has a number of subdisciplines, including aerodynamics, the study of gases, and hydrodynamics, the study of liquids. Wilbur Wright applied the principles of aerodynamics to calculate the forces on the aircraft and design the ideal wing shape. Outside of flight, fluid dynamics has a wide range of other applications, including determining how oil flows through pipelines and predicting weather patterns; it's even used in traffic engineering and road design, where traffic is treated as a continuous fluid.

Thermodynamics

The next area in which the brothers applied the principles of dynamics was thermodynamics. This term is derived from the Greek words *thermos*, meaning heat, and *dynamis*, meaning power. Thermodynamics is a branch of physics that studies how changes in temperature, pressure, and volume affect physical systems. Since heat means "energy in transit" and dynamics relates to "movement," thermodynamics explains the relationship between energy and movement. In this regard, when the Wright brothers were forced to design and build a light but powerful engine on their own, they had to understand how energy was generated and transferred to the engine to create the necessary velocity for their aircraft.

Thermodynamics developed in the early 19th century in the context of the increasing economic and industrial importance of the steam engine. Steam engines—the primary energy sources in locomotives, steamships, steam tractors, and the steam turbine, which was used for generating electricity—were essential building blocks of the Industrial Revolution. In 1824, Nicolas Léonard Sadi Carnot, a French mathematician and engineer known as the father of thermodynamics, published "Reflections on the Motive Power of Fire," a treatise on heat, power, and engine efficiency. This marked the beginning of thermodynamics as a modern scientific discipline. However, the actual term *thermodynamics* was not coined until 25 years later, in 1849, by Lord Kelvin, after whom the Kelvin scale of temperature was named.

Group Dynamics

Group dynamics are a social application of the thermodynamic theories, and it is the next area of influence on the Wright brothers. Group dynamics is a branch of the social sciences focusing on how groups interact. Group dynamics contends that individual behavior will differ depending on individuals' current or prospective connections to a group. Desires to belong to or to identify with a group tend to produce distinct attitudes that enable the influence of a group to become strong, even overwhelming individual judgment and actions. Group dynamics also may lead to changes in the behavior of a person when he comes before a group, and affect the behavioral pattern of a person vis-à-vis the group. Increasingly, group dynamics are being studied to understand how groups of people, such as work teams, juries, sports teams, and online communities, interact and make decisions.

When Octave Chanute, a fellow aeronautical pioneer, invited Wilbur to speak to the Chicago-based Western Society of Engineers after the disappointments at Kitty Hawk in 1901, it was a strong message of respect by an esteemed group of peers. The culture of that group was one of both adventure and analytics, and it reinforced Wilbur's own proclivities toward these same characteristics. In fact, had Wilbur not received the invitation to speak to this group—one that shared and reinforced his values—manned flight may have been delayed for years.

Laureus—
The Power of Sport to Change the World

"Sport has the power to change the world.
It has the power to inspire. It has the power
to unite people in a way that little else does.
Sport can awaken hope where there
was previously only despair."
—*Nelson Mandela, Laureus World Sports Awards, Monaco, 2000*

Laureus is the Latin word for laurel, the universal symbol for victory in sports. It is also the word for a group of the world's most dynamic leader-athletes who are devoted to promoting sports as a tool for social change. Specifically, the Laureus World Sports Academy is 41 legendary sports leaders from five continents who have all volunteered to support projects, raise funds, and draw public attention to and work to overcome some of the world's greatest social challenges, including poverty, homelessness, war, violence, drugs, discrimination, racism, and AIDS. Members with whom I have spoken talk reverently about Laureus, its bold aspirations, and the impact it is starting to have.

Collectively, the academy's members have achieved remarkable sporting feats, including 41 Olympic gold medals, 32 major golf titles, 6 NBA world championships, 6 Soccer world cups, 15 world motorcycling titles, 817 test match wickets, 24 National Football League records, 4 world figure skating titles, 8 world judo championship titles, 2 rugby world cups, 420 touchdown passes, 11 Triple Crown wins (horseracing), 11 Tour de France titles, 23 windsurfing titles, 34 Grand Slam tennis titles, and 2 Formula One world titles. The Laureus members discussed in this book include:

ACADEMY MEMBER	SPORT	COUNTRY
Sebastian Coe	Track and field	United Kingdom
Sean Fitzpatrick	Rugby	New Zealand
Michael Jordan	Basketball	United States
John McEnroe	Tennis	United States
Martina Navratilova	Tennis	United States
Jack Nicklaus	Golf	United States

CHARISMA VERSUS DYNAMISM

When thinking about the prototypical leader, it is common to picture someone who has personal magnetism, executive presence, and an abundance of self-confidence—charisma, in other words. Charisma is often considered the distinctive leadership attribute. After all, charismatic leaders are those who influence others to do what they want them to do. It is easy to use the word *dynamism* interchangeably with *charisma*.

However, while charisma and dynamism share some common linguistic bloodlines, they should not be confused. The characteristics are fundamentally different, and they come from dissimilar places. Investigating how they each fit into the English language demonstrates why dynamism is the characteristic to aspire to, the attribute to embody, and the value to live by. Likewise, the same analysis illustrates why charisma, while seductive, can easily lead one astray.

Consider the definition of charisma:

CHARISMA \ KƏ ' RIZ MƏ N. A PERSONAL ATTRACTIVENESS THAT ENABLES ONE TO INFLUENCE OTHERS.

Some of the greatest leaders in history, from John F. Kennedy and Ronald Reagan to Martin Luther King Jr., have been the embodiment of charisma. People were drawn to them. Indeed, their personal attractiveness, their appearance, their communication style, and their carriage enabled them to influence others on a historic scale.

Charisma, however, also enabled others to lead entire populations in disastrous directions. Adolf Hitler, with the aid of his elaborately produced rallies and propaganda films, is exhibit number one. Mao Tsetung, the exploiter of nearly a billion Chinese, employed charisma and ruthlessness to lead the Cultural Revolution and cripple three generations of Chinese in the process. Many of today's fanatical extremist regimes are similarly led by individuals whose charisma attracts followers, even if their wish is for others to forsake the otherwise universal respect for life.

In contrast, many great leaders have achieved extraordinary

accomplishments with an utter lack of charisma. Abraham Lincoln, for one, is well known to have been quiet, thoughtful, even boring. But his act of conscience and courage led to emancipation and brought an end to slavery in the United States. Mohandas Gandhi, better known by the name his followers gave him, Mahatma—"Great Soul"—was the father of India's independence from Great Britain. His passion for social justice and his belief in nonviolent revolutionary social change were manifested with quiet calm and resolve, not charisma. And Orville and Wilbur Wright, the modest bicycle shop owners from Dayton, Ohio, were about as far away from the typical leader as imaginable. What they lacked in charisma, they more than made up for with their devotion to a momentous idea and the intelligence and dogged determination to pursue it until it worked.

Dynamism can be exercised with *or without* charisma. Dynamism is an inherently positive force that enables progress individually and collectively.

Having now completed this book *and* graduated from Father Guido Sarducci's Five-Minute University, you now have both the intellectual underpinnings of dynamism firmly established as well as the principles, stories, and strategies to help you put them into practice. It's up to you to go out and pursue The Dynamic Path.

Notes

CHAPTER 1

pp. 1–5: Sources for the section on Bill Bradley: James M. Citrin interview with Bradley; *Values of the Game,* Bill Bradley (Broadway Books, 1998); *A Sense of Where You Are,* John McPhee (Farrar, Straus and Giroux, 1965); http://en.wikipedia.org/wiki/Bill_Bradley.

pp. 10–15: Section on Mary Wittenberg: Citrin interview with Wittenberg; www.time-to-run.com/marathon/newyork; www.ingnycmarathon.org; *Running Times* magazine, October 2001; www.nycgovparks.org.

CHAPTER 2

p. 19: Louise Ritter's quote is from *The Olympians' Guide to Winning the Game of Life*, compiled by Bud Greenspan (Stoddart, 1997).

p. 20: "Why Do Athletes Win at Business?" *Leadership by Example*, James M. Citrin, Yahoo! Finance, July 19, 2006.

pp. 20–21: "Masters of All Universes," *The Wall Street Journal*, September 22, 2006.

p. 22: Section on Arthur Ashe: *A Hard Road to Glory: A History of the African American Athlete*, Arthur Ashe (Warner Books, 1998); www.laprensa-sandiego.org/archieve/february07-03/ashe.htm.

p. 26: For the statistics on leadership: *The Five Patterns of Extraordinary Careers*, James M. Citrin and Richard A. Smith (Crown Business, 2003).

p. 28: "How to Manage Like Joe Torre," *Fortune*, April 30, 2001.

pp. 29–30: Section on Jeffrey Immelt: Citrin interviews with Immelt.

p. 30: Newton's first law of motion: *The Physics Classroom*, www.glenbrook.k12.il.us/gbssci/phys/class/newtlaws/u2l1b.html.

pp. 31–32: Section on Tiger Woods: Citrin interview with Dr. Bob Rotella; "Tiger Woods Up Close and Personal," *60 Minutes*, CBS, March 26, 2006; www.tigerwoods.com; http://en.wikipedia.org/wiki/Tiger_Woods.

pp. 33–34: Section on Bud Greenspan: Citrin interviews with Greenspan and his colleague Cassandra Henning; *100 Greatest Moments in Olympic History*, Bud Greenspan (General Publishing Group, 1995).

p. 33: "Fame as Motive: A Search That Never Dies," Benedict Carey, *The New York Times*, August 22, 2006.

CHAPTER 3

pp. 37–41: Section on Billie Jean King: *The Autobiography of Billie Jean King*, Billie Jean King with Frank Deford (Granada, 1982); Donna Lopiano quote is from National Women's Hall of Fame, www.greatwomen.org; *The Rivals: Chris Evert vs. Martina Navratilova, Their Epic Duels and Extraordinary Friendship*, Johnette Howard (Broadway Books, 2005); Evert quote and general background are from "Billie Jean King: Portrait of a Pioneer," *HBO's Sports of the 20th Century*, 2006; www.USTA.com; Citrin conversation with King.

p. 38: For the history of Title IX and statistics of girls playing high school sports in the United States: "Playing Fair: A Guide to Title IX in High School and College Sports," Women's Sports Foundation, October 8, 2001; www.womenssportsfoundation.org/cgi-bin/iowa/issues/geena/record.html?record=829.

p. 38: Statistics on participation in high school sports: *Morbidity and Mortality Weekly Report*, Centers for Disease Control and Prevention, U.S. Department of Health and Human Services, www.cdc.gov/mmwr/preview/mmwrhtml/mm5538a1.htm; *The NFHS Participation Figures Search Survey*, National Federation of State High School Associations, www.nfhs.org/custom/participation_figures.

pp. 40–41: Section on Mia Hamm: Citrin interview with Hamm; www.womenssportsfoundation.org; www.miafoundation.org.

pp. 41–42: Section on Grant Hackett: Citrin interview with Hackett; http://en.wikipedia.org/wiki/Grant_Hackett; http://en.wikipedia.org/wiki/Kieren_Perkins.

pp. 44–46: *Now, Discover Your Strengths*, Marcus Buckingham and Donald O. Clifton (The Free Press, 2001).

pp. 47–49: Section on Jerry Green: Citrin interview with Green.

pp. 52-53: Citrin interview with Eric Heiden.

p. 55: Citrin interview with Sean Fitzpatrick.

p. 55: "US Job Satisfaction Declines," press release, The Conference Board, February 23, 2007.

p. 56: Citrin interview with Pete Dawkins.

p. 57: Citrin interview with Dr. Aimee Kimball.

pp. 52, 54–58: Quotations at the beginning of each subsection: *The Olympians' Guide to Winning the Game of Life*, compiled by Bud Greenspan (Stoddart, 1997).

CHAPTER 4

p. 62: "What It Takes to Be Great," Geoffrey Colvin, *Fortune*, October 30, 2006.

pp. 62–63, 73: K. Anders Ericsson, department of psychology, Florida State University; "The Role of Deliberate Practice in the Acquisition of Expert Performance," K. Anders Ericsson, Ralf Th. Krampe, Clemens Tesch-Römer, *Psychological Review* 100, no. 3(1993): 363–406.

pp. 63-69: Section on Lance Armstrong and Chris Carmichael: Citrin meeting and interview with Lance Armstrong; Citrin interview with Chris Carmichael; *Every Second Counts*, Lance Armstrong with Sally Jenkins (Broadway Books, 2003).

p. 70: "The Role of Deliberate Practice in the Acquisition of Expert Performance," K. Anders Ericsson, Ralf Th. Krampe, Clemens Tesch-Römer, *Psychological Review* 100, no. 3 (1993): 363–406.

p. 71: *The Greatest Tennis Matches of the Twentieth Century*, Steve Flink (Rutledge Books, 1999).

p. 71: *On Being John McEnroe*, Tim Adams (Crown, 2003).

pp. 74–76: Citrin interview with Bob Rotella; *Golf Is Not a Game of Perfect*, Robert J. Rotella with Robert Cullen (Simon and Schuster, 1995).

CHAPTER 5

pp. 79–81: Citrin interviews with John Newcombe.

p. 81: Citrin interview with Lance Armstrong and Mark Gorski.

pp. 83-85: For section on the truth about winning: Citrin interview with Tom Veneziano; *The Truth About Winning*, Tom Veneziano; © Tom Veneziano.

pp. 85–87: Citrin conversation with Terry Orlick: *In Pursuit of Excellence: How to Win in Sport and Life Through Mental Training*, Terry Orlick, (Human Kinetics, 2000).

p. 88: *The Olympians' Guide to Winning the Game of Life*, compiled by Bud Greenspan (Stoddart, 1997).

p. 89: Citrin interview with Dr. Bob Rotella.

pp. 90–92: For section on Joan Benoit-Samuelson: Citrin interview with Benoit-Samuelson; Maine Women's Hall of Fame, www.uma.edu/libraries.html; Women in Sports, www.makeithappen.com.

p. 93: Data on athlete compensation and endorsement income from www.forbes.com.

pp. 94–95: For more on meeting and exceeding expectations and differentiating yourself in the workplace, see "Pattern Four, Differentiate Using the 20/80 Principle of Performance," *The Five Patterns of Extraordinary Careers,* Citrin and Smith.

pp. 96–99: For section on Tiger Woods and Michelle Wie: Citrin interview with Dr. Bob Rotella; www.tigerwoods.com; http://en.wikipedia.org/wiki/Tiger_Woods; www.missmichellewie.com; www.thefreedictionary.com/champion; www.classicbands.com/rollers.html.

CHAPTER 6

pp. 101–2: Citrin interview with Emmitt Smith.

pp. 104–6: Section on Senator George Mitchell adapted from Citrin's column on Yahoo! Finance, *Leadership by Example*, April 25, 2006.

p. 107: "Do College Sports Really Strengthen Character?" Gordon Marino, *The Wall Street Journal*, August 31, 2006.

pp. 107–9: Section on Steve Case: Citrin interview with Case.

pp. 109–10: *In Praise of Athletic Beauty*, Hans Ulrich Gumbrecht (Belknap Press of Harvard University Press, 2006).

p. 110: "Fall from Grace: Tragic Heroes of Sports," Ron Claiborne, *ABC News*, August 6, 2006.

pp. 111–12: Section on Roger Staubach: www.henrysmiller.com/history; www.famoustexans.com/rogerstaubach.htm; Citrin interview with Staubach.

pp. 112–13: Section on Bjorn Borg: *On Being John McEnroe*, Tim Adams (Crown, 2003); "Memories for Sale," *Tennis*, May 2006.

pp. 115–18: Section on Terry Bradshaw: Citrin interview with Bradshaw; www.foxsports.com.

CHAPTER 7

pp. 123–29: Section on Arnold Palmer: Citrin interview with Arnold Palmer; historical information on The Golf Channel is from Comcast Cable Networks; www.arnoldpalmer.com; conversations with Doc Giffin and Jed Hughes— Spencer Stuart partner and leader of sports recruitment practice, member of Latrobe Country Club, and friend of Arnold Palmer and Doc Giffin for many years; "Arnold Palmer Gives $2 Million to Pitt in Battle Against Cancer," David Templeton, *Pittsburgh Post-Gazette*, May 3, 2006; www.pgatour.com/company/pgatour_history.html.

pp. 130–36: Section on Tony Hawk: Citrin interview with Tony Hawk; Citrin conversations with Bobby Kotick, co-chairman and CEO, Activision;

www.tonyhawk.com; www.tonyhawkfoundation.org; "How Tony Hawk Stays Aloft," Mark Hyman, *BusinessWeek*, November 13, 2006.

pp. 139–41: Definition of benevolent leadership adapted from *The Five Patterns of Extraordinary Careers,* Citrin and Smith.

pp. 141–43: Section on Marvin Lewis: Citrin interview with Marvin Lewis; www.bengals.com.

pp. 146–47: *Executive Intelligence: What All Great Leaders Have*, Justin Menkes (HarperCollins, 2005).

pp. 149–50: *Career Warfare: 10 Rules for Building a Successful Personal Brand and Fighting to Keep It,* David D'Alessandro (McGraw-Hill, 2003).

pp. 150–52: *You're in Charge, Now What?,* Jim Citrin and Thomas Neff (Crown, 2006).

pp. 152–54: Section on Howard Schultz: Citrin interviews with Howard Schultz; *Pour Your Heart into It: How Starbucks Built a Company One Cup at a Time*, Howard Schultz and Dori Jones Yang (Hyperion Books, 1997); www.starbucks.com; www.myprimetime.com (Great Entrepreneurs series).

pp. 154–59: Section on Sean Fitzpatrick: Citrin interviews with Sean Fitzpatrick; *Peak Performance: Inspirational Business Lessons from the World's Top Sports Organizations*, Clive Gilson, Mike Pratt, Kevin Roberts, Ed Weymes (Texere, 2000); Sean Fitzpatrick profile by Lindsay Knight for the New Zealand Rugby Museum, www.allblacks.com.

CHAPTER 8

pp. 161–63: *Gates of Repentance: The New Union Prayer Book for the Days of Awe* (Central Conference of American Rabbis, 1978); New Year's resolutions based on a widely cited study conducted at the University of Washington in 1997 but still applicable today.

pp. 162–71: Section on Colin Powell: Citrin conversations with Colin Powell; www.americaspromise.org; www.kpcb.com; *My American Journey*, Colin Powell with Joseph E. Persico (Random House, 1995).

p. 172: Citrin interview with Tony Hawk.

pp. 172–74: Citrin interview with Lance Armstrong.

CHAPTER 9

pp. 179–81: Section on Wilma Rudolph: www.espn.go.com/sportscentury/ features/00016444.html, by M.B. Roberts; http://en.wikipedia.org/wiki/ Wilma_Rudolph; *Wilma*, Wilma Rudolph (Signet, 1977).

pp. 182–83: Section on Joan Benoit-Samuelson: Citron interview with Benoit-Samuelson.

pp. 184–88: Section on Magic Johnson: www.magicjohnson.org/about_us.php; www3.babson.edu/events/foundersday/johnson.cfm; "The Magic Moment," Peter Richmond, *GQ*, November 2006; conversations with Howard Schultz, chairman, Starbucks Coffee Company; Richard A. Smith, CEO, World 50; Barry Wade, chief operations officer, ZMagic.

pp. 191–95: Section on Bono: Citrin meetings with Bono; "Why Would a Rock Star Want to Talk to Me?" Robert J. Barro, *BusinessWeek*, July 16, 2001; "The Statesman," James Traub, *The New York Times*, September 18, 2005; www.joinred.com/manifesto.asp.

pp. 196–98: Section on Archie Griffin: Citrin interview with Griffin; www.greatsportsrivalries.com; www.bucknuts.com/osuhistory/ heisman_archiegriffin.htm; "Beyond the Gridiron: The Life and Times of Woody Hayes," a documentary co-production with Crouse Entertainment Group and WOSU-Columbus, Ohio, © The Duncan Group.

CHAPTER 10

pp. 199–205: Section on Buzz Aldrin: Citrin interview with Buzz Aldrin; www.buzzaldrin.com; *Reaching for the Moon*, Buzz Aldrin (HarperCollins, 2005); www.nasa.gov; www.space.com.

APPENDIX

pp. 209–10: Online Etymology Dictionary, www.etymonline.com; http:// en.wikipedia.org/wiki/Leibniz.

pp. 210–15: "The Wright Brothers and Their Decision to Fly," *Profiles in Audacity: Great Decisions and How They Were Made*, Alan Axelrod (Sterling Publishing, 2006).

pp. 217–18: Section on Laureus: Citrin interview with Sean Fitzpatrick; www.laureus.com.

pp. 219–20: *The Future and Its Enemies: The Growing Conflict over Creativity, Enterprise, and Progress*, Virginia Postrel (Touchstone, 1999).

Acknowledgments

I am very fortunate to have been able to work with so many great people over the past 3 years to make this book become a reality. First, I would like to thank Jeremy Katz, the best editorial and thought partner anyone could ever be so fortunate to work with. I would also like to acknowledge my literary agent, Rafe Sagalyn, who was a critical influence on how this book ultimately took shape; he took a bet on me a decade ago and has been a friend, partner, and valued advisor ever since. Similarly, Karen Steinegger, my executive assistant, has been a trusted partner in all aspects of my professional life over the past 13 years. A true friend as well as a colleague, she made all of the logistical and scheduling arrangements that made such a complex project run smoothly. Jordan Brugg, another valued Spencer Stuart colleague, has been a core part of this book since the very beginning. An increasingly expert student of leadership and performance in his own right, Jordan played an important role as a shaper of ideas; a researcher into even the most obscure corners of academia, medicine, and psychology on peak performance; and a highly entrepreneurial arranger of interviews. Anne Schmitt, another Spencer Stuart colleague, was a skilled editor and proofreader of the first overall draft of the manuscript. To help design the charts in the book, I am very grateful to Ann Williamson and Katie Staun for their excellent work.

This has been my first time publishing with Rodale, and it has been a fabulous experience. CEO Steve Murphy has instilled inside the organization a high-performing culture of editorial excellence bolstered by innovative marketing. He also was the very first person to whom I mentioned the concept of this book in July 2004. From that moment on, he encouraged me to be bold about engaging with the most-renowned champions and highest-performing leaders in the world. I also greatly appreciate the dedication and excellence of Nancy Hancock, Rodale's vice president and executive editor of health and wellness books. She has been simultaneously encouraging and demanding, challenging me to reach ever deeper to extract the most important insights from my research and to communicate them to readers in the clearest and most engaging way possible. Finally, the expanded Rodale team, including Andrew Malkin, Jenna Alifante, Amy Kovalski, Beth Davey, Cindy Ratzlaff, Karen Neely, Francesca Minerva, Bob Niegowski, Chris Rhoads, and Susan Eugster, have been the highest-quality professionals in the business as well as enthusiastic supporters of this book.

I would like to thank Mark Holcomb, editor of my *Leadership by Example* column at Yahoo! Finance. Having Mark hold my feet to the fire each fortnight has given me an outlet to explore many of the ideas and clarify my thinking about many of the subjects in this book and generate feedback from the column's broad readership. I also appreciate the encouragement from Keith Ferrazzi, CEO of marketing consulting firm Ferrazzi Greenlight, to not be too reticent about weaving some first-person narrative into the book. And Etienne Boillot, one of my closest friends for the past 25 years, gave me exceptionally incisive and helpful comments on the manuscript.

Each and every day, I feel fortunate to be a member of one of the great professional firms in the world, Spencer Stuart. I would like to thank my partners, colleagues, and friends around the world for creating a professional environment as close to the ideal of excellence, performance, and creative freedom as anyone could ever dream of. In particular, I would like to thank our managing partner, David Daniel; our chairman, Kevin Connelly; our chief financial officer, Rich Kurkowski; and the extended management team for their support. I would also like to thank Ben Machtiger, Spencer Stuart's ingenious chief marketing officer, who has been a continuous supporter in the development, marketing, and promotion of this book.

Of special import, I'd like to thank each and every person who helped arrange or invested their valuable time in the valiant effort to arrange the interviews and meetings that were the lifeblood of this book. Specifically, thanks go to Jordan Brugg in securing the interviews with Buzz Aldrin, Chris Carmichael, and Dr. Aimee Kimball; Rick Smith, founder and CEO of World 50, in securing the meetings with Lance Armstrong and Bono and working to enable me to speak with Magic Johnson; Tony Vinciquerra, CEO of Fox Networks Group at News Corporation, in securing the interview with Terry Bradshaw; Tom Neff, my Spencer Stuart partner, friend, mentor, and co-author, in securing the interview with Pete Dawkins; Arlen Kantarian, CEO of USTA's Professional Tennis, in inviting me to the US Open to sit with Chris Evert and for his efforts to help me meet John McEnroe; Joe McCollum, chief HR officer at EMI Music PLC, for introducing me to Sean Fitzpatrick; Cassandra Henning, a leader in the Olympic Movement, for her dedicated efforts to enable me to meet Bud Greenspan, speak with Lord Sebastian Coe, and interview Eric Heiden and Joan Benoit-Samuelson; Jed Hughes, my Spencer Stuart partner and leader of our sports management practice, in securing the interviews with Archie Griffin and Arnold Palmer; Neil Martin, my former Spencer Stuart partner and president of Swimming Australia, for arranging the interview with Grant Hackett; Rick Dudley, CEO of Octagon Sports, for facilitating the interview with Mia Hamm; John Mitchell, my Spencer Stuart partner, for his dedicated efforts to have me spend time (on the golf course!) with Michael Jordan; Harvey Schiller, chairman, Global Options, for introducing me to Billie Jean King; Dave Calhoun, CEO of Nielsen (formerly VNU), for introducing me to Marvin Lewis; Steve Murphy, CEO of Rodale, for his efforts to connect me with fellow Rodale author Martina Navratilova; Bill Dorman, former CEO of Dorman Cheese, for enabling me to spend time with John Newcombe; Jackie Arends, my Spencer Stuart partner, for paving the way for me to meet Colin Powell; Gil Stenholm, my Spencer Stuart partner, for introducing me to Dr. Bob Rotella; David D'Alessandro, former chairman and CEO of John Hancock, for setting up the interview with Juan Antonio Samaranch; Kneeland Youngblood, CEO of Pharos Group and one of the best corporate directors in America, for arranging my interviews with Emmitt Smith and Roger Staubach; Tom Daniels, my Spencer Stuart partner, for arranging and joining me in the interview with Mary Wittenberg; and David Daniel, my Spencer Stuart partner and the CEO of our firm, for inviting me to the Masters to enable me to walk along with Tiger Woods.

In addition, I'd also like to express my love and appreciation for my family. My brother, Jeffrey, sister, Nancy, and parents, Hal and Glenna, have each been more enthusiastic and engaged in this book than any others. Finally, my wife, Gail, and our children Teddy (17), Oliver (15), and Lily (12) have been consistent supporters, constructive critics, and models of patience during what has been a seemingly never-ending stream of research and writing.

Thanks, one and all.

About the Author

JAMES M. CITRIN is one of the world's leading executive search consultants and an expert on leadership and success. He is a senior director and member of the Worldwide Board of Directors of Spencer Stuart. Since joining Spencer Stuart in January 1994, Citrin has completed more than 350 executive and board director search assignments. Notable placements include:

▶ **CEOs** of Yahoo!, AOL, Nielsen (formerly VNU), Univision Communications, Starwood Hotels & Resorts Worldwide, Eastman Kodak, Hertz, Motorola, Motion Picture Association of America, BSkyB, Reader's Digest, Primedia, Gartner, L.L. Bean, Ziff-Davis, Kinko's, Holiday Inn Worldwide, Westin Hotels & Resorts, UPromise, Panavision, Sirius Radio, and the Markle Foundation

▶ **Board directors** for Microsoft, Yahoo!, Gap, Eastman Kodak, Ingram Micro, Starwood Hotels & Resorts Worldwide, Rodale, Blockbuster Entertainment, Akamai Technologies, Corporate Executive Board, Priceline, and Harrah's Entertainment

▶ **CFOs** of Microsoft, Viacom, Yahoo!, Activision, Expedia, Discovery Communications, Akamai Technologies, BBN Technologies, and the National Football League, among many others

Citrin's previous books are *You're in Charge, Now What?* (Crown Business, 2005), *The Five Patterns of Extraordinary Careers* (Crown Business, 2003), *Zoom: Navigating the Road to the Next Economy* (Doubleday, 2002), and *Lessons from the Top: The Search for America's Best Business Leaders* (Doubleday, 1999). He has coproduced and hosted special series based on the books for CNN's *Lou Dobbs Tonight* (September 2003) and CNBC's *Squawk Box* (January 2005). Citrin has appeared on *The Today Show*, *Good Morning America*, and CBS's *The Early Show* and has been interviewed by all major national print, television, and radio outlets. In addition, he writes the popular biweekly column *Leadership by Example* for Yahoo! Finance.

Prior to joining Spencer Stuart in 1994, Citrin was director of corporate planning at The Reader's Digest Association. Before that, he spent 5 years with McKinsey & Company in the United States and France, serving as a senior engagement manager. Earlier, he was an associate with Goldman, Sachs & Company, and spent 3 years as a financial analyst with Morgan Stanley.

A 1981 Phi Beta Kappa graduate of Vassar College with a BA in economics, Citrin has served as a member of the Vassar Board of Trustees since 1999. He earned an MBA from the Harvard Business School, graduating with distinction in 1986.

Thanks to *The Dynamic Path*, Citrin was honored to receive an invitation from the United States Olympic Committee to become an adjunct professor at their newly created Olympic University, a groundbreaking program of leadership development based on the principles of the Olympic Movement. He lives in Connecticut with his wife, Gail, and their three children, Teddy, Oliver, and Lily.

Index

Boldface page references indicate illustrated concepts.